PRAISE FOR S

Aside from the textbooks themselves, this is the most useful book I have read in my academic career. Without *Study Smart*, I would not have survived this academically rigorous school.
— Lindy Harper
     Senior at St. Andrew's Academy

Dr. Seel is right. It is "patently absurd that students are expected to spend twelve to sixteen years in school and nowhere in their curriculum are they given a course on the tools needed to become a successful student." This book answers that deficit and opens the door to real education, not just test prep. In doing so, Dr. Seel gives practical hope to struggling students. His compassionate but honest exploration of the attitudes and habits necessary for students to succeed is long overdue and is equally valuable for the academically advanced who want to learn, not just maintain a GPA.
— Leslie Y. Moeller
     Chairman of the Board, Society for Classical Learning

As a former student of Dr. Seel and a secondary school teacher who taught his course on study skills, I know firsthand that *Study Smart* can have a profound impact on how students experience their own learning. The rich, practical guidance Seel offers transforms the challenging task of being a student into an elevated and joy-filled calling—a vocation—to realize one's fullest potential in service to God, the common good, and the world.
— Jesse Bates
     COO, Valor Public Schools,
     Former student and athlete of Dr. Seel

An educator at heart and by calling, David John Seel wants Christian students in Christian schools to excel. Like the determined coach who sees potential, Seel identifies the disciplined practices that can become habits of the heart leading to mastery and ultimately to wisdom.
— Denis Haack
Founder & Director, Ransom Fellowship

In today's world, we need well-informed, educated young men and women who are prepared to leave the hallowed halls of their schools equipped to impact the world for eternity. This book can help them do that.
— Timothy P. Wiens
Ed.D., Head of School, Mount Paran Christian School

"Most education today is fraught with both bad philosophy and bad practice. David John Seel is a master educator, and in this most recent little book he has set forth a much-needed corrective to both sides of the dilemma. In a very brief manner, he has articulated the aims and why of education, coupled with very important practical guidance for students. Students and parents take note: ignore Seel's counsel to your own peril and disadvantages or follow it to your great profit and delight."
— Paul Wolfe, Ph.D.
Head of School, The Cambridge School of Dallas

After 25 years of college teaching, I have found that the students who are most successful, those who are capable of engaging deeply with the curriculum, all have one thing in common, disciplined study habits. Dr. Seel's book provides a marvelous opportunity for all students, especially those who struggle in their studies, to improve those habits which will help them not only in school but also in life. I highly recommend this book.
— Chris Swanson, Ph.D.
President, Gutenberg College

STUDY
SMART

A CHRISTIAN GUIDE
TO ACADEMIC SUCCESS

David John Seel, Jr.

To all my students,

from whom I have learned much and owe more

TABLE OF CONTENTS

YOU'VE BEEN CHEATED

If you're like most kids, you don't have a choice when it comes to school. For many it's a drag. You survive only because of your friends and sports. Actually, learning is low on your list of priorities. You get by because you've learned how to do the minimum amount of studying needed to avoid maximum alarm from your parents. You sit in the back row when you are able. You avoid eye contact with the teacher when questions are asked. Being unnoticed is a learned social skill. Among your friends being academically smart is a liability, decidedly uncool. There is a certain pride in not doing well in school. And so you endure the boredom and the routine of the classroom with daydreaming, secretly texting on your phone or playing video games, and frequently checking the clock. Test days and report cards are dreaded speed bumps on the road to your social life and to the things you think matter. The vast majority of students in junior high and high school are exactly like you—getting by with the minimum amount of effort. You've tried to fit in quietly with this majority. But now you've been noticed!

A day of reckoning has come. Your grades have suffered, and in response someone has handed you this book to read. Reading it is just one more choice you didn't make yourself. No one likes to have a point of personal weakness highlighted. This is totally understandable. I was once exactly where you are now.

Your situation is not totally your fault, though. Most of you have been cheated by the adults around you and by the educational system that you are in. They have forced you to go to school, but they have done nothing to help you succeed in school. Smart kids barely need school. They would probably learn this stuff on their own. But you are different. For you schooling is a struggle and rarely fun. And so you endure the process each year moving to the next grade. But at some point, these low-grade patterns of academic rebellion catch up to you and the proverbial wheels fall off the wagon. Typically the failures of elementary schools show up in the eighth or ninth grade. You blame the school, the teachers, the textbooks, but you know that your heart has not been in this process of learning for a long time. Your academic struggles are the fruit of a choice you made years ago. It is easier to be angry with others… than to be honest with yourself.

There are secrets to learning. There are steps you can take that will make school easier and more rewarding—ways of doing more with less, studying smarter. If you follow the steps in this book, your grade average will improve by a letter grade in two semesters. It is almost guaranteed. Learning does not have to be a mystery. There are ways of getting more from the classroom and textbook. There are ways of reading that increase what you remember. There are ways of doing better on a test. The problem is that no one has bothered to tell you how to play this game in a way that enables you to succeed. Average ability students, like me, need all the help we can get.

You've probably dug yourself an academic hole. It will take some effort to get back on track. But this much is certain: if you follow the guidelines discussed in this book you will be able study smarter, you will begin to believe in your potential, and so will others. So let's get started together.

I was in school as a student for thirty-two years—twelve primary and secondary, four college, four masters, eleven doctorate, and one EMT certification—and I was not an academically able student. Over the course of these many years, I learned some tricks of the trade that made the process of schooling more productive. My aim here is to help you succeed by passing on to you the secrets of academic success that no one bothered to teach me along the way. The key is not to be smart, but to study smarter.

Here's how.

MY STORY

It seems patently absurd that students are expected to spend twelve to sixteen years in school and nowhere in their curriculum are they given a course on the tools needed to become a successful student. Granted, every student is different and there are certainly different learning styles. But there are also ways to make the learning process less opaque and less dependent on a purely hit-or-miss process. Schools are cheating their students by withholding this information.

The measure of a great school is not what they are able to do with exceptionally bright students, but with average-ability students who inherently struggle with confidence, motivation, and ability. I was just such a student. On my office wall is a framed copy of my first-grade report card from New York City's Collegiate School. This is a prestigious boys prep school in New York's Upper West Side famous for graduating John-John Kennedy. He would enter the school eight years after me. This report card is from March 1960, approaching the end of my first-grade year. Regarding reading, my teacher, Kathryn M. Merchant, wrote, "Johnny seems to like reading and he has a good ear for phonetic sounds. When he gives reading his undivided attention and his best effort, he reads well. Unfortunately, this is seldom the case. His concentration is poor, and he often loses his place. At this time, Johnny is reading below average first-grade level." I got top marks in shop and gym! Academic insecurity followed me through my schooling.

I attended a missionary boarding school in Daejeon, South Korea. At this school, students who had below B averages were required to attend supervised study hall in the library every school night.

This meant in practice that the school dunces were evident to everyone. I was one of those dunces. I didn't achieve a B average until the second semester of my junior year in high school. It was around this same time that I realized that I needed glasses in order to be able to read the blackboard in class. There was no school testing on the mission field, but it later became evident that I was dyslexic before dyslexia was cool. I gradually compensated for my academic insecurities and dyslexia—except for math—and went on to triple-major in college and receive a master's and doctorate degree. I was overcompensating for my intellectual insecurity all the way through. None of this was without effort and some trauma.

So when I became a college preparatory school headmaster, I had a particular passion and sympathy for insecure struggling students. It was my desire to help them succeed. While I was leading a particularly rigorous academically-oriented single-track Advanced Placement school, I developed these study secrets, which were then routinely taught to students in the eighth grade. It was my belief that average-ability students when given the right resources are able to do more than they believe that they can do. And this was a school filled with average-ability students—students who on the Independent School Entrance Exam averaged a 6 out of 9. When I left, the average SAT score for the school was 1358 with the typical student taking five AP courses with an 85 percent pass rate.

I often reminded my students that every spring in the NFL there is a day called Black Monday, when failing NFL coaches are fired. These are men who never took a snap, caught a pass, or made a tackle. They never stepped on the field during a game, but they were held accountable for the success of their team. Every good teacher should feel the same degree of accountability for the success of their classes as does a professional NFL coach for his team. To that end I was determined to help my students succeed.

And I did not lower my academic standards. I was known as a demanding teacher and a hard grader. Some of my AP European History exams took two blue books to complete. But I could also be found studying with my students at Starbucks until midnight preparing for their final exam or AP test. My strongest aspiration was the genuine success of my students.

Later I would put this same philosophy into practice coaching crew. In 2005 two athletes from a boys' crew team of six rowers from a small Christian school of 150 students in Texas won the bronze medal in the double at the United States Junior Rowing Championship in Cincinnati. This was a competition against all of the elite prep schools in the nation. I am convinced that we do not push our students hard enough to maximize their full potential. Greatness is possible, but not without pain and diligence. I've often thought that if we taught in our classroom with the same passion, skill, and standards as we coach Texas high school football or crew... all would be well.

This book is designed to give average-ability students a leg up on their academic competition, to enable them to achieve their potential as a student, and to do so with less failure and pain. There are no guarantees, but this is where all students must begin.

David John Seel, Jr., M.Div., Ph.D.
Founding former headmaster
The Cambridge School of Dallas
A classical, Christ-centered college preparatory school

HOW TO USE THIS BOOK

This book was originally taught as a one-semester course to eighth graders. In general, this material is appropriate for middle and high school students. Most of the "Further Reading" sections are aimed at the high school student, parent, or teacher. When taught as a course, these readings may be the source of essay questions by the upper-level students as they wrestle with the concepts presented. Study skills are learned best when they are incorporated into the requirements of homework assignments on a regular basis, such as a student gets credit for reading, if the reading assignment is underlined according to the guidelines in this book, papers are submitted with their original typed outline, and the like. Teachers should reinforce the regular use of good study skills in their homework expectations.

With over twenty years working in prep school and classical Christian school administration, I have written widely on these topics. Included in the Further Reading sections are some of these essays, which are probably more useful for the parent and teacher by way of educational background than to the student, except for the upper level secondary school student. They suggest a pedagogy of study. They defend the "why" behind the "what" of the study skills being presented.

Parents should encourage their child's school to teach and reinforce study skills as a routine part of their curriculum. It is unfair to the student to expect them to learn effectively without those responsible for their learning giving them the tools to learn ahead of time.

When a student uses the book alone, I recommend that the student discuss each chapter with a parent upon its completion. *The book is only useful if it is applied.* At the end of each section the student has the option to commit to a short-term and long-term action step. If a student can regularly apply these principles over the course of thirty days, study skills will become more routine and natural to their learning process. This is the goal: for these study skills to become second nature to the student and accomplished without conscious thought throughout their academic career.

It is also important for the parent to reinforce the application of these study skills just as a school might when it is taught in that context. Have the student write up an agreement between the student and the parent to accomplish this over the course of one semester.

As in all things, attitude is everything. Start by making small incremental goals and build on them from there. Big success comes after a series of small successes.

Chapter One

THE LEARNING PROCESS

'Love the Lord your God with all your heart and with all your soul and with all your mind.' This is the first and greatest commandment. — Jesus

Study is the total of all habits, determined purposes, and enforced practices that the individual uses in order to learn. — William Armstrong

No one can become really educated without having pursued some study in which he took no interest—for it is part of education to interest ourselves in subjects for which we have no aptitude. — T.S. Eliot

Everything is interesting if you go into it deeply enough. — Richard Feynman

Lack of aptitude is a symptom, not a disease. The real trouble has its basis in poor work habits, in ineffective techniques, and lack of background information. — William Armstrong

What is Learning?

In America, if you don't go to school you can be arrested. Education is mandated from kindergarten to the twelfth grade. Truancy rates remained constant between 2002 (10.8 percent) and 2014 (11.1 percent). Rates were highest among older youth, females, and Hispanic youth. For all racial/ethnic groups, truancy was significantly correlated with alcohol and marijuana use, fighting, the propensity to take risks, and lower academic engagement and school grades. Older students get easily distracted by other priorities—relationships, money, and addictions—and have the ability to push back against their parents. They have mastered the skill of rebellion, of flying just below their parents radar of concern and outrage.

The widespread legal obligation for towns and villages to provide free education did not evolve until the late nineteenth century and truancy was born in such legislation as the Education Act of 1872. Over and above the obligation within such legislation for local government to provide school buildings and teachers, there was also a counterpart requirement for the children to actually attend them, and within this the legal concept of truancy was born. It is a relatively new educational phenomenon.

It is my view that this well-intentioned law, while understandable, is counterproductive to the wider educational task. *We should do away with mandatory education. The reason for this is that one can only learn what one desires to learn. Forcing kids to attend school when they don't want to is a waste of time for everyone involved.*

Desire is everything. Mere presence in a school or classroom is no meaningful measure of whether real education is happening. William Armstrong puts his finger on this aspect of learning: "Do you want an education enough that you would work and pay for it yourself? If you cannot find within your heart and soul the desire to learn, then you need not expect help from without. The teacher is the guidepost for the journey, but the journey is yours." *You will only be able to learn if you desire to learn. While it is the teacher's responsibility to make the subject interesting and relevant (not entertaining), it is the student's responsibility to get this information into their brain in a manner that enables sufficient recall and use long after the class has ended and the test given.*

This gets to the heart of the learning process. *Learning only happens when the student takes the initiative to repattern the information given.* Think of it as kneading bread dough. Even with the best ingredients, bread dough won't rise properly without being folded over and over to build up its structure. When it comes to learning, the student has to get their hands in the subject's dough and mix it thoroughly. This kneading can take many forms: summarizing the material, putting it into an outline, making a list, underlining the book, turning the material into song lyrics, and the like. This is something more than just letting the information passively wash over you. It involves getting your hands dirty. We will discuss the many ways this academic kneading can be done, but the basic theme is it involves the student rearranging the material in a manner that involves some form of bodily effort. Passively sitting in the presence of the material is not learning any more than sleeping with a tablet under one's pillow, a strategy allegedly attempted by King Charlemagne. The student has to take the information and put it into a meaningful pattern for themselves. Knead the dough.

Big Ideas
1. The *desire* to know is critical for all learning.
2. Learning involves personally *repatterning* the information ("kneading").

Two Types of Learning
In general there are two kinds of learning: training and transformational. The first deals with the "how" and is more technical and pragmatic. The second deals with "why" questions and is more abstract and theoretical. While it is true that students tend to be more oriented to one or the other, true learning always involves both.

1. Training involves learning to do something—usually involving a repetitive process to change or do something outside of yourself. I might teach you how to change the tire on a car. Every car might be a little different, but the skills and steps are all pretty much the same.

2. Transformational learning is learning aimed at changing you. The goal here is not to be able to do something, but to become a certain kind of student, a student with wisdom. The question here is not how to change a flat tire but knowing why tires go flat. This kind of learning is called the liberal arts. It aims to teach a person how to live or how to gain wisdom. "Why" learning is a deeper kind of learning than "how" learning.

It is one thing to be able to do something. It's quite another to know why you should do something. We need both kinds of learning if we are going to be truly educated.

Three Barriers to Learning
If learning is your goal, then you also need to be aware of barriers to achieving this goal. The first barrier is *coercion,* in that it removes any sense of personal responsibility from the student. As I have stated, mandatory education is a barrier to learning. Are you willing to learn even if you had to pay for it yourself?

The second barrier is *grades*. Grades are important as a measure of achievement, but they are not a meaningful motivation for learning. If grades become your extrinsic motivation, you will tend to cut corners and undermine the intrinsic motivation for wanting to learn for its own sake. "Is this going to be on the test?"—a question that teachers should never allow from their students—is a very different student motivation than "This is interesting."

The third barrier is *television*, video games, and social media because a heavy dose of these technologies will shorten one's attention span and become a substitute for reading. They will also give one the impression that the most meaningful medium of learning is entertainment. Philosopher Douglas Groothius writes, "Communications guru Marshall McLuhan coined the slogan, 'the medium is the message.' Taking his clue from the discussion of idolatry in Psalm 115, McLuhan remarked that, 'We become what we behold.' When we become habituated to a particular form of communication, our mentalities and sensibilities bear its mark." To develop a disciplined and learned mind we must pay attention to "what we behold." Too much TV will make it harder to learn Latin, because learning Latin demands close attention to details. You must limit those habits that will weaken your ability to learn—particularly those that shorten your attention span. If smoking makes it harder for you to be a good athlete, so too excessive television viewing makes it harder for you to be a good student.

The Christian Student's Calling
For the Christian student, learning becomes a calling, in effect, a spiritual responsibility as an expression of your obedience to God and his lordship over your life. To this end, the spiritual "why" of studying must become the deepest source of your motivation as a student. I recommend that you pray before doing your homework. You should also reflect on and memorize this description of a "Student's Calling."

"We study in order to understand God's good creation and the ways sin has distorted it so that, in Christ's power, we may bring healing to persons and the created order and, as God's image-bearers, exercise responsible authority in our task of cultivating the creation to the end that all people and all things may joyfully acknowledge and serve their creator and true king."

Understanding the Learning Process

There are known steps in the learning process for any subject.

1. You cannot learn what you do not love.
   Desire to learn is key.

2. All knowledge is based on previous knowledge.

3. Getting the BIG PICTURE is the main thing.

4. Master the generalities and the details will fall into place.

5. Knowledge is not learned until it is personally reorganized or repatterned—kneaded like dough.

6. In order to master kneading the dough, one must master the four basic skills of learning. This book is a primer on these four skills.
   - Listening
   - Reading
   - Writing
   - Memorizing

Guarantee

Any student who regularly applies the principles learned in this book to all their subjects is guaranteed to raise their GPA average one letter grade in two semesters. Studying well can make up for lack of brilliance. The process may be hard (let's not sugar coat it), but the results will be yours, lasting, and rewarding. These same disciplines will also translate into every other aspect of your life. Smart studying can raise one's grade one letter.

Big Ideas

1. You learn what you love.
2. Learning involves repatterning the information.
3. Transformational learning is the most valuable—learning for wisdom.
4. Avoid the barriers to learning with caution: coercion, grades, and television/media.
5. Adopt a spiritual motivation for studying. Adopt an attitude of prayer.
6. Master the four basic skills of learning: listening, reading, writing, and memorizing.

Action Steps

1. Short-Term: Develop a habit of praying before you do your homework just as you might pray before eating a meal.

2. Long-Term: Memorize the "Student's Calling."

A Student's Calling

"We study in order to understand God's good creation and the ways sin has distorted it so that, in Christ's power, we may bring healing to persons and the created order and, as God's image-bearers, exercise responsible authority in our task of cultivating the creation to the end that all people and all things may joyfully acknowledge and serve their Creator and true King."

MEMORIZATION BREAKDOWN

WE STUDY IN ORDER TO UNDERSTAND GOD'S GOOD CREATION

AND THE WAYS SIN HAS DISTORTED IT

SO THAT, IN CHRIST'S POWER, WE MAY BRING HEALING TO PERSONS AND THE CREATED ORDER

AND, AS GOD'S IMAGE-BEARERS, EXERCISE RESPONSIBLE AUTHORITY IN OUR TASK OF CULTIVATING CREATION

TO THE END THAT ALL PEOPLE AND ALL THINGS MAY JOYFULLY ACKNOWLEDGE AND SERVE THEIR CREATOR AND TRUE KING.

Students With Promise

The first question management guru, Peter F. Drucker, asks an organization to consider is "Who is my customer?" It is the same question that directors of admissions ponder? It is the same question embedded in the mission statements of the finest private schools from Roxbury Latin to Oregon Episcopal. What type of student is best served by a college preparatory education? Who are "students with promise"?

The answer to such a basic question reveals one's assumptions about human nature and the educational process. The story is told of a terrible train wreck. Locals gathered curiously around the tangled mass of derailed freight cars, as rescue workers struggled to identify a person caught in the debris. After anxious minutes passed, the sheriff yelled to the growing crowd, "It's OK. It's just a hobo." Out of the dust and smoke came a feeble but clear voice, "I's not a hobo. I's Jesse Smith." The intrinsic value of the individual—a person with a name—can never be taken for granted. SAT scores or Daddy's wallet cannot measure such value.

And yet, schools that seek to serve everyone soon find that they are serving no one. Not every applicant is best served by a private school. Some of the best schools accept only a third of those seeking admission. On what basis should an independent school decide—intellectual potential? Financial ability? Racial diversity? Geographic distribution? Who then are "students with promise"?

Students with promise are those whose lives are framed by a purpose *larger than themselves combined with a* passion *to serve that purpose.*

Education involves the embodiment of knowledge. Facts and formulas must be personally ingested, that is, made one's own. Money can buy proximity to learning, but money alone cannot buy an education. Wealth may acquire one libraries of leather-bound books or galleries of rare art, but affluence cannot buy one an educated mind. For all the books under his pillow, Charlemagne never learned to read. Great teachers may inspire, but when all is said and done, learning remains hard work—work that no one can do for the student but the student. French social theorist Pierre Bourdieu observes that learning requires "a labor of inculcation and assimilation, costs time, time which must be invested personally by the investor. Like the acquisition of a muscular physique or a suntan, it cannot be done second-hand." Learning is personal and must be embodied.

Here is the rub. The prevalent attitudes of youth culture weaken what this process requires. The premise of *consumerism*, that education like entertainment can be purchased whenever one wants, undermines the assumption of personal cost. The premise of *cynicism*, that meaning doesn't matter, undermines requisite personal motivation. Research shows that many young people are characterized by an "active pursuit of disengagement, detachment, fragmentation, and emotional numbness." The "Whatever Generation" is bored and adrift. Douglas Coupland's *Girlfriend in a Coma* depicts life for the postmoderns of the 90s as full of hollow diversions and roads not taken. As larger aims are never defined, individuals become who they are by default. Their dreams are forgotten… or are never formulated to begin with.

For such a young person, a private school education is an economic and educational waste, however high-minded the parents or capable the teachers. No, a student of promise is not one who has the economic resources to attend or even the intellectual acumen to excel, but one who has the purpose and passion to appreciate and seize the opportunity that such an education affords. There still remain many young people who care about AIDS victims, ecology, and the poor, who strive for excellence in music, art, and athletics, and who have not lost the idealism of youth for the consumerism and cynicism of pop culture. These are the ideal private school customers. These are students with promise. While fewer in number, they will shape things to come.

Three objections to this line of thinking come immediately to mind. First, a student who by middle or high school has a developing sense of purpose and a passion to pursue that purpose would do well in almost any educational environment. Are the best schools only for the best students?

Second, is not the discovery of a life purpose exactly what is developed during a child's maturation? Much of the identity exploration of adolescence lays the groundwork for a sense of life direction and moral engagement. Is it realistic to make this a major criterion of student selection?

Third, is it not just as much the responsibility of the school to instill the desire to learn as it is the student's responsibility to have that desire? Isn't it really a question of the chicken and the egg? Which comes first? Doesn't an emphasis on selecting students with purpose and passion abdicate the teacher's role in providing a stimulating and challenging educational environment, a classroom experience that fans into flame the smoldering ember of potential in each entering student with "sticky" instruction?

These objections have merit and provide balance to the argument presented here. However, the process of education itself demands acknowledging the responsibility of the student and making it a key factor in student admissions. It is the single greatest factor that makes the decisive educational difference.

For an educated mind cannot be bought. It has to be earned. Only the opportunity for education can be bought. It is a mistake to minimize the student's role in education. Teachers teach. Students educate themselves. Such an emphasis is far less elitist than typical criteria based on financial or intellectual resources. Drive and desire become *any* student's academic trump card.

From the first day of kindergarten, the best schools must seek to instill a sense of the student's educational responsibility as well as to inspire the student's desire to learn. While education is a dynamic partnership between teacher and student, the student remains the active partner. Education is more than simply transferring information. Rather, it is the embodiment of knowledge, which requires developing a love of learning. It is rarely achieved without the involvement of flesh-and-blood, caring teachers. For such a love is caught as much as it is taught, role-modeled as much as downloaded—a process that cannot be fulfilled in virtual reality. What is seen in and through the life of a teacher is what transforms learning from mere facts to infinite possibilities. James Madison states that at the end of the day, the key question is not "What did the student learn?" but "What has the student become?"

Education is not a passive process—something that is done *to* the student who simply shows up. Students who can most benefit from what independent schools offer are not the rich or brilliant, but those who care. This is precisely why "whatever"—the mantra of the disengaged—just won't make the grade.

Mastery Before Love

"My daughters don't have a love for learning," lamented the concerned mother. "Is something wrong with them or is something wrong with the school?"

This is an important question. What is meant by "a love of learning"? When does it happen in the educational process? These questions are particularly pressing on those who seek to develop "a love of learning coupled with a passion for Jesus."

The short answer is that the love of learning is the fruit of an education and is not its root. It's the end, not the beginning. Let me explain.

C.S. Lewis has a little known essay titled, "The Parthenon and the Optative." The Parthenon is a marvelous marble temple built between 447 and 432 B.C. The optative mood is a grammatical mood in Greek that indicates a wish or hope. The contrast is between a picture and a grammatical tense. Lewis begins,

> "The trouble with these boys," said a grim old classical scholar looking up from some milk-and-watery entrance papers, which he had been marking: "the trouble with these boys is that the masters have been talking to them about the Parthenon when they should have been talking to them about the Optative." Ever since then I have tended to use the Parthenon and the Optative as the symbols of two types of education. The one begins with hard, dry things like grammar, and dates, and prosody; and it has at least the chance of ending in a real appreciation which is equally hard and firm though not equally dry. The other begins in "appreciation" and ends in gush. When the first fails it has, at the very least, taught

the boy what knowledge is like. He may decide that he doesn't care for knowledge; but he knows he doesn't care for it, and he knows he hasn't got it. But the other kind fails most disastrously when it most succeeds. It teaches a man to feel vaguely cultured while he remains in fact a dunce. It makes him think he is enjoying poems he can't construe. It qualifies him to review books he does not understand, and to be intellectual without intellect. It plays havoc with the very distinctions between truth and error.

There is an important lesson here. One needs to engage in the hard work of learning a subject, before one can appreciate what one is studying. The love of learning does not happen at the beginning of a student's engagement with a discipline, but at the end. Virgil doesn't fascinate one like senior AP students, until one has learned the vocabulary and mastered the conjugations and declensions.

The day I climbed Mount Blanc in the French Alps was thirty-six hours after an avalanche on the same route of my ascent had killed two Germans. The day of my climb was a sunny cloudless day with spectacular views. From the top of Mount Blanc one could see the Matterhorn in Switzerland and the peaks of the Italian Alps. Getting to the top of this nearly 16,000-foot mountain was among the most difficult physical feats I have undertaken. Prior to that climb, I worked out almost three hours per day for six months. Immediately prior to the climb, I had cycled sixty miles-per-day for a week in Ireland. Yet the climb was still hard—breathtaking (in every sense of the word), I would say. I can show you the photographs. You can page through the books on the Alps that line my bookshelves, but it is fundamentally not the same as having been there and made the climb. The view from the mountaintop is not gained by short cuts or surrogate experiences. It has to be embodied. And so it is with learning.

Several years ago I took a group of seniors and their parents to the L'Abri Conference in Rochester, Minnesota. At an Italian restaurant called Victoria's, the group sat among reproductions of Botticelli and Michelangelo. Having just written a paper on these artists in AP Art History, two senior students discussed them with understanding and depth. David jumped up and quizzed Lauren on a specific Greek relief sculpture. Beyond the sculpture itself, they went on to describe the significance of the way it was framed. Lauren then mused on her recent visit to the Kimbell Art Museum in Fort Worth to see a Mondrian exhibit. "I never appreciated Mondrian until we studied him in class. I could identify his paints, but it was only lines and color," she said. "Now I understand the significance of what he was trying to express artistically. It's amazing." What would have been her response had she gone to the exhibition prior to studying Mondrian in class? What if the professor had asked her then, "Which painting do you 'love'?"

Two types of education: Parthenon and Optative. Love of learning does not mean a shortcut to effort. It does not mean entertainment. It means embracing the challenge of learning the first things first. Hillsdale journalism professor Tracy Simmons warns, "Before the young can know the dangers of soft teaching or the seductions of ignorance, non-knowledge gets planted and watered. And left unchecked, as it usually is, it will spread like bamboo." The Way of the Optative is different. It may not guarantee the ascent to appreciation; nonetheless it is the one way that weather-beaten mountaineers have tested and found to be reliable. We dare not stop at the foothills and stare affectionately at a picture from the summit and call it a day. We are too easily pleased. In the end, it is students who are cheated out of the thrill of mastery. Hesiod wisely reminds all aspiring students, "Before the gates of excellence, the high gods have placed sweat." The love of learning is a prize hard won. But it is worth the effort.

Chapter Two

MASTERING THE TEACHER

Give them not only noble teaching but noble teachers.
— Dorothea Beale

*The important thing is not so much that every child should be
taught, as that every child should be given the wish to learn.*
— John Lubbock

*What greater joy can a teacher feel than to witness a child's
success? — Michelle L. Graham*

*Good teaching cannot be reduced to technique; good teaching
comes from the identity and integrity of the teacher.*
— Parker Palmer

Three Tools of Learning

There are three basic tools of learning: time, textbooks, and
teachers. One must learn the skills to master each. We begin by
learning to master our teachers. Teachers are people. Popular film
and stage actress Phyllis Brooks rightly observed, "Teaching is
truth mediated by personality." Every teacher will have a different
personality. Mastering the teacher is essential for a student's
success. Teachers are people and naturally respond to a student's
appreciation, interest, and respect.

The first thing is to reframe our perspective on teachers. They are
not the enemy eager to give students a bad grade in order to ruin
their lives, but instead are a trusted ally and advocate for students'
success. There are two major factors that make a good teacher:

intellectual competence and relational connection. Every teacher scores higher or lower on one of these two variables. In general, elementary school teachers are stronger on connection than competence and high school teachers the reverse. The old insight "Students don't care how much you know until they know how much you care" gets at these two variables. Both are equally important.

Even the weakest teacher will generally know more than their students do and therefore deserves the respect of the student. Teaching is a uniquely difficult profession. It demands long hours. It has a high emotional cost. It requires balancing competing constituents, many of whom are generally disrespectful of the teacher: board members, administrators, parents, and students. Culturally, teaching is now a profession that is low in social respect and compensation. The combination of these factors can make teachers particularly sensitive to criticism to the point of being "prickly." It also makes them equally appreciative of appreciation, interest, and respect from the student. It is for these reasons that students can make a big difference in their connection with their teacher. There are always some subjective aspects to grading. It is always best to have the teacher on your side.

Every teacher is different. It is the student's responsibility to adjust to the teacher's teaching style, course expectations, and personality. You don't have to like a teacher to be able to learn from a teacher. This is the fallacy of the Yelp-like reviews of the website "Rate My Professor" that frames education as a consumer choice.

It is the best case when a teacher makes his or her presentation "sticky," so that his or her instruction is automatically easy to remember. Chip and Dan Heath defines a sticky presentation in their book *Made to Stick* as one that is:

- simple
- unexpected
- concrete
- credible
- emotional, and
- laced with stories.

But even if the teacher consistently violates these rules, it is still the student's responsibility to turn the class presentation into "sticky" notes useful for later recall.

Here are some ways that you can master your teacher.

1. Study the course syllabus – Before class have an expectation of what is going to be taught.

2. Listen for the daily lesson plan – "What am I expected to learn today?" Particularly listen for the *big idea* of today's class—the expected main take-away. Many exam questions come from the big ideas or ask the student to relate one big idea to another one. End each class with a summary of the big idea. If you are not clear about what it is, ask the teacher before leaving the class.

3. Develop a personal bond with the teacher – There are common student stigmas about being the "teacher's pet." But it is the student's responsibility to develop a bond with the teacher. Sit close to the front of the class. If in a Zoom class, keep your camera on. Raise your hand when asked to participate. Ask follow-up questions. Always push towards "why" questions. "Why is this lesson important?"

4. Evaluate the teacher –
   - Is the teacher's style formal or informal?
   - What kind of teaching tools does the teacher prefer to use in class? Handouts, whiteboard, PowerPoint, experiments?
   - What is the teacher's teaching style? How can you maximize it?
     - Lecture (Be sure to get the main point.)
     - Discussion (List the themes discussed and participate.)
     - Problems (What kind of problems are presented?)
     - Textbook (Is it the main source of the instruction or does the teacher use secondary sources?)
     - Handouts (Assume information on a handout is important.)
     - Whiteboard (What does he or she use the whiteboard for: core content, illustration, highlighting, additional questions to explore?)
   - How important is homework? (Recognize that neatness in doing one's homework immediately translates into your attitude toward the subject.)
   - How does the teacher do evaluations? (How often are quizzes and tests given? How might this impact your schedule for reviewing the material and your class notes?)

5. Establish the right reputation early – The teacher is like your boss on a job or coach on a competitive athletic team. Seek to demonstrate the following:
   - Seriousness about learning
   - Conscientiousness in small things
   - Interest in subject matter
   - Consistently preparation and organization

- Meaningful contributions in class
- Respectful attitude toward the learning process

6. Show gratitude – It is simple to say "Thank you" at the end of the class.

7. Never leave a class without knowing the "big idea" of the class. You might not understand it, but you'd better know what it was. If you are unsure, ask the teacher before leaving the classroom.

SAMPLE LESSON PLAN

Not every teacher will provide the student with the sample lesson plan. All good teachers have one. It is the student's job to figure out what it is, particularly the big idea or expected main take-away desired by the teacher for the class.

Western Civilization II or AP European History

Note the big ideas. Future essay questions will come from these understanding sections with the facts and dates being used as supporting evidence. Always get the big picture.

Theme: Reformation (1517-1560)

1475-1525 High Renaissance
1517-1550 Luther
1536-1560 Calvin
1534-1563 Henry's Act of Supremacy to Elizabeth's Thirty-Nine Articles
1545-1563 Council of Trent
1521-1556 Ignatius Loyola

Monday: Big Idea—New Monarchs (Rise of Charles V)

Knowledge
- Reason for Rise
- Key Players
- Key Rivalries
- Impact on Reformation

Skills
- Chronology
- Outlining

Big Idea – How Political and Religious Motivations Merge

Handouts
- Chapter Fact Sheet
- Historical Map of Period

Homework
- Read and outline "The Protestant Reformation"
- Memorize Fact Sheet (due Friday)

Tuesday: Big Idea—German Reformation (Martin Luther)

Knowledge
- Cause of the Reformation
- Luther's Insight into Justification
- Reasons for Success
- Assessment of Consequences

Skills
- Chronology
- Outlining

Big Idea – Authority from Councils to Conscience

Reading—"Luther at the Diet of Worms"

Handout—"Consequences of the Reformation"

Homework
- Read and outline "The Protestant Reformation"
- Memorize Fact Sheet (due Friday)

Wednesday: Big Idea—International and English Reformation

Knowledge
- Contributions of John Calvin
- Henry VIII's Break with Rome
- Elizabeth I Compromised Moderate Protestantism

Lecture: "The Reluctant Reformer"

Skill
- Note Taking
- Outlining
- Chronology

Big Idea —Basic Ecclesiology (Episcopal, Presbytery, Congregational)

Handout—"The Reluctant Reformer"

Reading—"Spiritual Exercises"

Homework
- Memorize Fact Sheet
- Read "Spiritual Exercises"
- Read and outline "Catholicism Reformed and Reorganized"

Democracy And Educational Standards

Democracy requires more than fireworks and hotdogs—it requires cultivating minds that can comprehend and wills that aspire to its core principles. Democracy requires education. But education is not democratic. Let me explain.

America is uniquely a nation established on ideas. From the Founders on, Americans have had a responsibility to reaffirm their commitment to concepts like freedom, equality, and human dignity—Thomas Jefferson's call for "a revolution every generation." This is more than the rote citing of the Pledge of Allegiance or the singing of the national anthem. Its demands are far greater. Democracy obligates its adherents to know what the ideals mean and to seek the virtues they require. "The pursuit of happiness" is not an invitation to a shopping spree. "Freedom" is not license—the behavior of "consenting adults."

Tracy Lee Simmons author of *Climbing Parnassus* writes,
> Americans view the Founding Fathers *in vacuo*, isolated from the soil that nurtured them. They're whitened statues, existing out of time, locked in greatness. But little doubt can there be that the years those men had invested at school and college with Greek and Latin—had prepared them optimally for the role they would play on history's stage…. Never have so many of the wise and well-read come together to do great things; never have book learning and practical experience combined to show

the ignorant and cynical forevermore what the human mind and spirit can do when properly formed. Such wisdom cannot be manufactured for the moment—nor can it be aped. It must be cultivated. And it has to come from somewhere. For the Founders it came principally from two places: the pulpit and the schoolroom.... Early Americans didn't simply pray; they read books. These men were not, all of them, narrow religionists of legend. They were conversant with the world of ideas in ways few college graduates today could rival. They were also cultured. We forget—perhaps because we were never taught—that even some of those fierce, fiery preachers of the seventeenth and eighteenth centuries who pounded Bibles had also once pounded Latin paradigms in class.

While democracy requires educated citizens, it is important to remember that education itself is not democratic. When democracy becomes the measure of all things, democracy loses. For it to be strong, democracy must be nurtured from sources outside of itself—principally, as noted by Simmons, from the pulpit and from the classroom. It is the fruit of other labors; it is not the root. Wrongly understood, the democratic spirit can be its own undoing.

It is commonly observed that postmoderns do not like standards—except perhaps their own when they are in power. And as a general rule, Americans do not like elites. Elites are something we allegedly left behind in the Old Country. Americans, since the populism of Andrew Jackson, resist hierarchy. Instead, egalitarian pragmatism courses through our veins. We celebrate the common man. We debunk greatness. Everyone is just as good, just as smart, and just as wise as the next. The only difference still acknowledged in a celebrity culture is fame. But this too is in reach of the average American by sharing his or her unmentionables on *The Jerry Springer Show*. Anything that reminds us that reality itself is hierarchical must be destroyed. Our worship is man-centered; our wisdom is left to simple majorities. To this end we have allowed envy to be institutionalized and legitimized with patriotic purpose.

Henry Fairlie calls it "The Revenge of Failure."

> If we cannot paint well, we will destroy the canons of painting and pass ourselves off as painters. If we will not take the trouble to write poetry, we will destroy the rules of prosody and pass ourselves off as poets. If we are not inclined to the rigors of an academic discipline, we will destroy the standards of that discipline and pass ourselves off as graduates. If we cannot or will not read, we will say that "linear thought" is now irrelevant and so dispense with reading. If we cannot make music, we will simply make noise and persuade others that it is music. If we can do nothing at all, why! we will strum a guitar all day, and call it self-expression. As long as no talent is required, no apprenticeship to a skill, everyone can do it, we are all magically made equal.

Fairlie describes the democratic spirit perverted. The Founders were elites. Their education was serious. And we will never appreciate their unique accomplishments unless we too aspire to and honor genuine greatness. Egalitarianism wrapped in the flag destroys the ideals that make democracy possible. It also destroys education and its ability to serve democracy. We do well to remember the words of C.S. Lewis:

> Equality has no place in the world of the mind. Beauty is not democratic; she reveals herself more to the few than to the many, more to the persistent and disciplined seekers than to the careless. Virtue is not democratic; she is achieved by those who pursue her more hotly than most men. Truth is not democratic; she demands special talents and special industry in those to whom she

gives her favors. Political democracy is doomed if it tries to extend its demands for equality into these higher spheres. Ethical, intellectual, or aesthetic democracy is death.

Vanity Sizing

Vanity sizing is now a common practice in the clothing industry. The term refers to the sizing down of apparel. For example, consider a pair of jeans that would be considered a size 8 by the standards set forth by national sizing charts. Now imagine that you are a size 8 and would like to try on this particular pair of jeans, but you find, much to your delight, that they are too big. Many clothing manufacturers take advantage of this sizing method in order to make their customers feel good about being able to wear a smaller size. But, of course, what has changed is not the customer's waist, but the manufacturers' standard.

In a world where relativism is largely assumed and belief in absolutes is looked down on as intolerant, every standard is malleable, every deadline a mere suggestion, and every person an exception to the rule. Consumerism coupled with notions of self-esteem reinforces this softening of standards. "I deserve to feel good about what I have bought." Bit by bit, standards are adjusted to consumer wants rather than consumer's wants adjusted to standards. The self rather than the standard reigns supreme.

Vanity sizing has found its way into education. Rather than maintaining objective standards of mastery, administrators and schools adjust the standard to fit the child under the pressure from parents. Everyone goes away happy—and ignorant. "What is generally sought in the production of minds is easy pleasure and information without labor," Alexis de Tocqueville wisely observed about America.

Few moderns believe in objective value—that some things are really true, good, and beautiful and other things are not. It is an uphill battle. Few support standards. Few embrace accountability. It's a problem even at the nation's most elite institutions. "The historical role of centers of learning has been to preserve standards and protect enduring achievements from the wind and fire of momentary political and populist whim," writes *New York Times* columnist William Henry. But this is no longer the case. Consider the example of Harvard University Professor Harvey C. Mansfield, the William R. Kenan Jr. Professor of Government. He became notorious by bucking the grading inflation common among other Harvard professors. He gave his students two grades: the first, the grade he believes they deserved and the second, a grade consistent with the inflated grade common among Harvard undergraduates, the so-called "ironic grade." About half of Harvard's students get an A-minus or above, while only 6% receive a C-plus or lower. It's "ironic," he explains, because it is a lie. "What's behind it I think is the evil notion of self-esteem in American education. You see it in higher education as well as in high school and elementary education, where it's attracted more attention. But in higher education it's there, and it's just as powerful. It says that the end of education is to make a student feel good about him or herself, and to make him feel confident and feel empowered. And this is at the cost of applying strict standards of judgment about how well that student has done. So it always leads—it inevitably leads—to the relaxation of academic standards."

The Economist observed wryly, "Living on a diet of junk grades is like living on a diet of junk food. You swell up out of all decent proportions without ever getting any real nourishment. And you end up in later life regretting your disgusting habits." It's true. Ross Douthat, author of *Privilege: Harvard and the Education of the Ruling Class*, looks back at his Harvard education with regret. "It was only afterwards, when the perpetual motion of undergraduate life was behind me, that I looked back and felt cheated."

There are many things in schools that have institutionalized this standard-weakening attitude—from the tracking of students to college recommendations. Yet to be excellent, we need standards. C.S. Lewis observed, "Unless the measuring rod is independent of the thing being measured, we can do no measuring."

Some may think this is a hard-edged attitude lacking grace. But God doesn't grade on the curve either, otherwise the cost of grace would not have been the death of his son. The fact that many in our day no longer believe in objective value does not change the fact that reality is so ordered. Few lessons are more important to teach our children than this fact. School is like golf. We need par in order to play the game well. James Schall writes, "Classrooms are in a sense like golf courses, where the standard of par looms over our performances, good or bad, no matter how much we have beaten the others in the foursome with whom we are actually playing. The highest things require our attentive efforts no matter how satisfied we are with what is less than the highest. The imperfect is not the perfect and ought not to be confused with it. The highest things do call us out of ourselves, even in our happiest moments." Par makes us better golfers. Standards make us better students. Objective value makes us better persons. So much for vanity sizing—the mirror never lies.

Chapter Three

STAYING ORGANIZED

Good order is the foundation of all things.
— Edmund Burke

For every minute spent organizing, an hour is earned.
— Benjamin Franklin

Organizing is what you do before you do something, so that when you do it, it is not all mixed up. — A.A. Milne

Success is not always achieved by hard work alone; but mix it with a little bit of organization and a little strength from God above and you'll have a winning recipe.
— Russel Honore

One of the first skills a student must learn is how to organize their *study materials* and how to keep them neat and accessible. Merely cramming textbooks, papers, and supplies into your backpack or locker is not staying organized. This means proactively keeping all the classroom notes and handouts from each course together. This also means keeping track of one's assignments, including possibly keeping a calendar. Organization is perhaps the one thing that separates a good student from a failing one. It is also a skill that you can easily accomplish even with average ability. Every office supply store has tools that are useful for achieving this goal. There is no right or wrong way to accomplish this and you can figure out your own system. Minimally, I would have an accordion folder for each course. I would try to keep the daily handouts from each course in chronological order. While it is not necessary to go over the top, some system is always necessary.

Of secondary importance is a regular *study area*. This is not a sofa or bed! It should be a well-lit desk with a comfortable chair. You should get in the habit of studying in the same quiet place every day. This area should be just as organized and neat as your backpack. Ideally, this needs to be in a separate quiet place, not the kitchen table.

Your *locker* should not be used as a storage locker or one's main base of operations. Rather it should be used only as a temporary holding area so that you are not having to carry all of your books and supplies to every class. The wrong use of a locker is the reason so many students are disorganized and why so many notes and handouts are lost. *The main base of your student operations needs to be your study area at home, not your locker at school.* Your home study area is the base of operations, the backpack is the transportation device, and your locker is only the temporary holding area for parts of what is in your backpack during the school day.

The home study area, backpack, locker, and classroom are the four areas that the student needs to be managed and are the typical source of confusion and disorder. Learn to manage each of these appropriately. This foundation of organization will make a big difference in your grades. Typically, students go from being in a one-room classroom in elementary school to a multi-room educational environment in junior high and high school separated by periods. They generally make this complex leap without any instruction, practice, or guidance.

Under the best of circumstances this is a confusing and disorganizing step for the young student. Add to this the practical matter of finding the restroom, figuring out when you can go, and the location of your next class—much less remembering your locker combination—adds to the stress. There is almost no help given to students to make this adjustment. I went from a one-room schoolhouse of ten students to a junior high of one-thousand students. The memory of this adjustment still freaks me out. There will be some inevitable stress; but you should work from the outset to stay organized as it is the foundation of all other successes.

1. Organization is the most important variable in a student's success.

2. Assignment Book

3. Courses
    - Books
      – Do not use another student's books.
      – Do not leave your books in Lost & Found.
    - Handouts
    - Class notes
    - Homework
    - Tests
    - Memory cards

4. Study Area – strategic base of operation at home. If the home environment is too chaotic, then use a local library as your base of operation.
    - Regular location
    - Desk / chair
    - Bookshelves
    - File drawers
    - Light
    - Supplies
    - Whiteboard
    - Clock
    - Computer
    - Calendar

5. Locker – tactical base of operations (do not use for storage)
   - Class schedule
   - Organize by periods
   - Backup supplies (paper and pens)

6. Backpack – Transportation only. Unpack at locker and desk each day.

7. Classroom
   - Assignment book
   - Textbook
   - Notes file
   - Homework file
   - Handout file
   - Supplies

Big Idea
1. Staying organized is the foundation to all academic success.
2. Have a regular study area at home that serves as your base of operations.
3. The structure of school is designed to make you disorganized. Develop a system to counter this tendency and stick with it.
4. Do not use your locker as your base of operations or storage unit.

Action Steps

1. Short-Term: Plan out an organizational system.

2. Long-Term: After a month of school, have a parent review your plan in operation.

Further Reading

Donna Goldberg with Jennifer Zwiebel. *The Organized Student: Teaching Children the Skills for Success in School and Beyond* (Touchstone, 2005).

Laurie Chaikind McNulty. *Focus and Thrive: Executive Functioning Strategies for Teens: Tools to Get Organized, Plan Ahead, and Achieve Your Goals* (Rockridge Press, 2020).

Chapter Four

How to Listen

It is paradoxical that listening is the easiest way to learn but the hardest study skill to master. —Anonymous

Most people do not listen with the intent to understand; they listen with the intent to reply. — Stephen R. Covey

There's a lot of difference between listening and hearing. — G.K. Chesterton

The word "listen" contains the same letters as the word "silent". — Alfred Brendel

Listening is a challenge for two reasons. First, we tend to think we are more important than the other person and are therefore more interested in formulating our reply than in understanding what is being said. Pride is a barrier to listening. Listening starts with humility. This is a matter of character.

Second, we think four times faster than we speak, so it is easy to outpace what is being said. To listen well, we have to adopt strategies to slow down our thinking to match the pace of what is being said. This is a matter of mastering the skill of listening. The first barrier is a choice. The second is a learned skill.

1. The Challenge of Listening
   Listening is a passive activity. Hearing is an active one. The goal of listening is hearing, and the goal of hearing is understanding. Hearing is not an activity of the ears, but

of the mind. It is a critical study skill. It involves finding a way to slow the mind down to stay with the speaking pace of the other person. This can be done in a number of ways: taking notes, interjecting knowing remarks, and asking follow-up questions.

"Now to learn to think while being taught presupposes the other difficult art of paying attention. Nothing is more rare: listening seems to be the hardest thing in the world and misunderstanding the easiest, for we tend to hear what we think we are going to hear, and too often we make it so. In a lifetime one is lucky to meet six or seven people who know how to attend: the rest, some of whom believe themselves well-bred and highly educated, have for the most part fidgety ears; their span of attention is as short as the mating of a fly. They seem afraid to lend their mind to another's thought, as if it would come back to them bruised and bent." — Jacques Barzun

"Listening, like reading, is primarily an activity of the mind, not of the ear or the eye. When the mind is not actively involved in the process, it should be called hearing, not listening; seeing, not reading." — Mortimer Adler

- Loss of ability (oral–hardest vs. written–hard vs. visual–easiest)
- Lack of humility (giving up the stage in a social setting)
- Lack of instant replay
- Lack of activity (Responding in the process of listening: "Really." "Is that right!")
- Lack of associated control (4X or "driving a car without brakes")

- Focus or slow down
- Anticipate or drive around
- Annotate or drawing a map

2. Asking the Right Questions
"The good listener, like the good reader, is a demanding listener, one who keeps awake while listening by having in mind the questions to be asked about the speech being listened to." — Mortimer Adler

- What is the whole talk about?
- What is the main idea?
- What are the main points?
- Are the speaker's conclusions right or wrong?

3. Taking Good Notes
"Since listening to a speech or any other form of oral discourse is intrinsically more difficult than reading a book or an essay, it is even more necessary to put pen or pencil to paper in the process. Skillful listening involves skillful note-taking, both while the speech is going on and after it is over, when one reviews one's notes and reflects on them." — Mortimer Adler

- Big idea
- Conclusion
- Key terms
- Underlying premises
- Main points (skip the illustrations)
- Implications

4. Reviewing and Rewriting Notes

Big Idea

1. Listening requires hearing and hearing requires slowing your mind to the pace of the speaker.
2. Good hearing almost always requires taking notes. Listen with a pen in hand.
3. Good listening takes practice.

Action Steps

1. Short-Term: Practice taking notes of from one of these two TED Talks. Write down the big idea, the main points, and the implications.

   How to retune your ear for "conscious listening" with Julian Treasure's "5 Ways to Listen Better": https://www.ted.com/talks/julian_treasure_5_ways_to_listen_better?language=en#t-450875

   Listening lessons from a deaf percussionist Evelyn Glennie: https://www.ted.com/talks/evelyn_glennie_how_to_truly_listen/

2. Long-Term: Take notes from a Sunday sermon and share them with your family afterwards. Did you get the main points?

Further Reading

Natasha Daniels. *Social Skills Activities for Kids: 50 Fun Exercises for Making Friends, Talking and Listening, and Understanding Social Rules* (Rockridge Press, 2019).

Chapter Five

DOING HOMEWORK WITH LESS TIME AND PAIN

A genius is a talented person who does his homework.
— Thomas A. Edison

Any human being whatsoever, though practically devoid of natural gifts, can penetrate to the kingdom of truth reserved for genius, if only he longs for truth and perpetually concentrates all his attention upon its attainment... under the name of truth I also include beauty, virtue, and every kind of goodness... the conviction that had come to me was that when one hungers for bread, one does not receive stones.
— Simone Weil

Training is doing your homework. It's not exciting. More often than not it's tedious. There is certainly no glory in it. But you stick with it, over time, and incrementally through no specific session, your body changes. Your mind becomes calloused to effort. You stop thinking of running as difficult or interesting or magical. It just becomes what you do. It becomes a habit. — Jack Edmonds

All students have a love/hate relationship with homework. Homework is like practicing before a game. The quality of the game play is always reflected in the quality of the practice. Those who succeed on the field in competition are those who love the hard work and monotony of practice. *Homework is where you demonstrate to yourself and others your true attitude toward school and learning. This is where you take ownership of your goals. It is where the game is won.*

As long as you are a student, you can never say that you don't have homework. Minimally, you should organize and review your notes from the day's lesson for ten minutes per class—which can easily take an hour. Review the "big ideas" from each class of the day.

How you do your homework is what really indicates the quality of the student in attitude toward learning, retention of knowledge, and quality of academic performance.

1. Schools should have a meaningful homework policy and make sure that the work assigned is clear in its learning objectives and reasonable in its time demand. Certainly honor or advanced placement courses will require a greater homework load. Students with demanding course loads do need to make the most of how they spend their scheduled homework time.

2. Homework underscores the student's personal commitment to learning.

3. Homework is a test flight. It should raise additional questions for the student to ask the following day.

4. Homework serves learning, not doing.

5. Homework is for organizing material for review as well as reviewing the day's big ideas in each course.

6. Homework takes planning and preparation— determining the appropriate location in which to do it as well as assessing the difficulty of subject, the length of assignment, and resources needed for the assignment.

7. Homework Guidelines: Follow these guidelines and you will be learning more in less time. Studying smarter, not studying longer.

- Always begin with prayer. Homework is a spiritual discipline directly related to the "student's calling."
- Do not sit with friends or "talkers" during study hall.
- Use study halls at school to accomplish your easiest assignments.
- Do not leave school until your Assignment Book is reviewed so that you know exactly what you need to take home.
- Do not do homework collaboratively with other students unless collaboration is intrinsic to the assignment. When a homework assignment is done with friends, the homework subject becomes friends.
- Do not do homework with the phone on, in earshot of a television, or with instant messaging activated.
- Do homework in the same quiet place at a well-lit desk at the same time each day—develop a routine and habit.
- Do not do homework with music with lyrics—unless it's Mozart or other baroque composers quietly in the background—headphones are recommended for the best effect. Listening to Mozart will make you smarter. Never have the television on while you are studying. This is a cosmic no-no—parents should be asked to enforce this guideline.
- Map out a plan—sequence the homework assignments and provide a rough time estimate for each assignment.
- Start with hardest assignment first. Reading is generally harder to do when tired. Writing is easier. Do the most exacting assignments first (i.e., fact

review, languages or Latin, math, history, English, and theology)

- Do Fact Review every day—use a parent right after dinner (15–30 minutes) to go over vocabulary, dates, or other memorized facts.
- Take disciplined breaks—but no more frequently than every 45 minutes. Give yourself rewards when each assignment is finished.
- Learn to take catnaps or "power naps"—of no more than 15 minutes per hour.
- Use weekends strategically to do big assignments that enable you to get ahead—such as read a novel, write a paper, do a project, or type the week's notes. This requires mapping out these larger assignments and getting them on your calendar ahead of time. Meeting these kinds of deadlines is a routine part of adult life.
- Master keyboarding. Typing is now probably more important than script. If you haven't taken a typing course, do so immediately. The rewards are incalculable.
- Always organize material so that it is ready for review when it is time for studying for a test or exam. Studying for a test is not the time to organize the material or learn it for the first time, but the time to review what you have previously learned.
- Begin studying for a test at least one day prior to the test so that questions that come up during the review process can be discussed with the teacher the day before the test.
- A student always has homework. Never tell a parent, "I don't have any homework tonight." Use the average amount of time studying each night even if all the assignments are completed. *Homework is about learning, not doing. Learning is about getting the information into your mind so that it stays.* Organize.

Review. Write sample test questions. Take the daily SAT review question. Never study less than two hours per night—this is a minimum (approximately 15–20 minutes per subject).

- Avoid television viewing as much as possible during the school week—limit viewing to one or two shows per week as a reward for completing assignments. Television is both addicting and makes you dumb. It's counterproductive to your academic goals as a student.
- Write up a homework contract with your parents—plan, expectation, accountability, and reward. It is especially helpful to obligate your parents to 15 minutes per night of fact-reviewing across all subjects.
- Avoid marathon sessions (four hours is generally the most a person can effectively study at any one time), and all-nighters are generally counterproductive, though every teacher has probably had one or two all-nighters in their academic career. From experience, they don't work!
- Give the teacher feedback if the homework load appears too heavy or is too confusing to be completed. But note that such concerns are only credible if they come from a student who works efficiently and consistently. If your reputation is that you do not use study halls well or are inconsistent in doing homework or turning in assignments on time, then your complaints about the homework load will not and should not be taken seriously.
- There is a big jump in homework loads between the sixth and seventh grade, between the eighth and ninth grade, and between the eleventh and twelfth grade. It will gradually increase from two to four hours per night, which is why it is necessary to learn to study well and efficiently in the earlier grades.

8. Learning languages are often the most difficult subjects. Classical schools tend to require some study of Latin or Greek. Latin and Greek are inflected languages, while English is not. An inflected language is one in which the words of the language are comprised of roots, stems, and inflections, or endings. The Roots remain relatively stable, and the inflections change depending on what job the word is doing in the sentence. It is for this reason that the study of Greek and Latin demand a high degree of attention by the student. This is also why a student's performance in Latin is the best single measure of their effective homework habits. *Latin and Greek are the best measure of a student's study skills because of what they demand to learn well:*

- Latin requires a daily investment.
- Latin as a subject is detailed and exacting.
- The study of Latin is cumulative and developing.
- Latin vocabulary requires constant daily memorization.
- The discipline of review is necessary even when it is easily avoided.
- In Latin only long-term memory counts, so thirty days of memory is usually required to know something for life.
- Latin is rigorous—it is the "brain surgery" of a high school curriculum.
- Latin is of all disciplines the most transformative in the life of a student.
- If a student can master Latin, he or she can effectively master any other subject. *Latin is not intrinsically hard; rather it is intrinsically demanding.* It is the ultimate test of a student's academic discipline and good study habits.

Big Ideas
1. Homework is the personal measure of a student's ownership of the learning process.
2. Homework must become a daily routine.
3. Homework is about managing time effectively.
4. Homework should be done in a place that maximizes your ability to learn well and avoid distractions.

Further Reading
Simone Weil. "Reflections on the Right Use of School Studies with a View to the Love of God," *Waiting for God* (Harper Perennial Modern Classics, 2009).

FURTHER READING

Study As A Sacrament

The life and works of Simone Weil (1909–1943) are not well known among contemporary Christians. A French Jewish philosopher living in the shadow of Nazi Germany, Weil converted from Marxism to Christianity without ever actually being baptized into the church. She refused to be baptized in order to reach non-believers. She thought public church membership would pose a barrier to her Marxist friends. Weil is sometimes described as a "saint for the churchless."

A migraine sufferer from childhood, she like so many other Christian mystics before her, learned the spiritual value of suffering. ("He whose soul remains ever turned in the direction of God while the nail pierces it, finds himself nailed on to the very center of the universe. It is the true center... it is God.")

A brilliant classical philosopher and teacher, she is sometimes compared to the melancholy Danish philosopher Søren Kierkegaard. Weil wrote an essay in 1942 for her spiritual director and confessor, Father Perrin, when he was appointed Superior of the Dominican House in Montpellier and had frequent contact with students from the local university. The short essay, "Reflections on the Right Use of School Studies with a View to the Love of God," bears our consideration.

"The key to a Christian conception of studies is the realization that prayer consists of attention. It is the orientation of all the attention of which the soul is capable toward God," she writes. Studies develop the disciplined faculty of giving attention. It is an advantage to the task of learning attention if one lacks a natural interest or ability in a given subject. The harder it is the better. Consider the challenge of a proof in geometry. "It does not even matter much whether we succeed in finding the solution or understanding the proof," she suggests, "although it is important to try really hard to do so. Never in any case whatever is a genuine effort of the attention wasted.... Without our knowing or feeling it, this apparently barren effort has brought more light into the soul."

How foreign these words sound in the ears of a modern Christian—or secondary school student. We see no value in struggle, no achievement in failure, no benefit to suffering. And so, we remain both intellectually and spiritually flaccid. We do not sustain effort, accustomed as we are to instant gratification and immediate results. Yet that which is most transformative of the body and soul is only achieved by sustained effort—concentrated attention. Its fruit is more than academic. It is spiritual.

We learn to attend to God in prayer. Weil writes, "Students must therefore work without any wish to gain good marks, to pass examinations, to win school successes; without any reference to their natural abilities and tastes; applying themselves equally to all their tasks, with the idea that each one will help form in them the habit of that attention which is the substance of prayer." Homework should always be begun with prayer and should be done with the realization that the hard work it entails will give one the power to attend not only to Latin, but to the Logos himself.

But what of the failed exam? Here Weil, both the student and teacher writes, "When we force ourselves to fix the gaze, not only of our eyes but of our souls, upon a school exercise in which we have failed through sheer stupidity, a sense of our mediocrity is borne in upon us with irresistible evidence. No knowledge is more to be desired. If we can arrive at knowing this truth with all our souls, we shall be well established on the right foundation."

Humility before truth is the attitude of the Christian student. Apparently, the self-esteem movement has it just backwards.

We need to approach our studies with both humility and attention.

If there are academic virtues derived from studying, then we do well to guard against whatever undermines their fulfillment. Two barriers come readily to mind—grade inflation and television. The assignment that costs one nothing and the grade that has no bearing on mastery rob the student of the spiritual value that can only be achieved by serious intellectual concentration. Pain is part of the process, as in athletics. This realization is not popular with parents or students today. But to pretend otherwise is to shortcut the transformative nature of schooling.

And then there is television and smart phones—the agents of inattention. The rapid pace of television images makes sustained reflection increasingly difficult and thought undesirable. Theologian Douglas Groothius warns, "God's word—'Be still and know that I am God'—simply cannot be experienced through television." As cigarettes are to a marathon runner, so television is to a serious student.

Instead, if we learn to approach our studies with humility and attention, we will see every Latin translation and every geometry proof as training in giving attention to God and our fellow human beings. Inattention is to be preoccupied with the self. Attention is the ability to give oneself to the other—whether vocabulary words, the teacher, or God. In the end, both love and prayer demand attention. Weil concludes, "Every school exercise, thought of in this way, is like a sacrament."

How Music Makes You Smarter

Have you ever noticed how your favorite music can make you feel better? New research studies now show how music can make you smarter too! Recently, a book called *The Mozart Effect* by Don Campbell has condensed the world's research on all the beneficial effects of certain types of music.

Some of the hundreds of benefits of music include the following:

- *Improves test scores*
- *Cuts learning time*
- *Calms hyperactive children and adults*
- *Reduces errors*
- *Improves creativity and clarity*
- *Heals the body faster*
- *Integrates both sides of the brain for more efficient learning*
- *Raises IQ scores 9 points (research done at University of California, Irvine)*

In 1996, the College Entrance Exam Board Service conducted a study on all students taking their SAT exams. Students who sang or played a musical instrument scored *51 points higher on the verbal portion* of the test and an average of *39 points higher on math.*

Major corporations such as Shell, IBM, and Dupont, along with hundreds of schools and universities use music, such as certain baroque pieces, to cut learning time in half and increase retention of the new materials.

According to the research outlined in the book, musical pieces, such as those of Mozart, can *relieve stress, improve communication and increase efficiency.* Creativity scores soar when listening to Mozart.

Music activates the whole brain and makes you feel more energetic. In the workplace, music "raises performance levels and productivity by reducing stress and tension, masking irritating sounds and contributing to a sense of privacy," says Campbell, author of *The Mozart Effect.*

Mr. Campbell has compelling new evidence to show how music, used properly, has calmed students with such problems as ADHD and even helped autistic children. He says, "forty-three of the world's largest industrial companies provide music to their employees." Dupont used a music listening program in one department that cut its training time in half and doubled the number of people trained. Another corporation using music found that clerical errors decreased by one-third.

Dr. Georgi Lozanov, the renowned Bulgarian psychologist, developed a methodology for teaching foreign languages that used baroque music with a beat pattern of about 60 beats per minute. Students learned in a fraction of the normal time. In a single day, one half of the normal vocabulary and phrases for the term (up to 1,000 words or phrases) were learned. In addition, an added benefit was the students had an average of 92 percent retention of what they had learned!

Dr. Lozanov has proven conclusively that by using certain baroque pieces, foreign languages can be mastered with 85–100 percent effectiveness in thirty days, when the usual time is two years. Students learning with the baroque music were able to recall their second language with nearly 100 percent accuracy even after they had not studied it for four years!

For many years, with thousands of students, the Center for New Discoveries in Learning has been evaluating the use of music both in the classroom and while students study. We have found that students using Mozart and certain baroque pieces (recorded at about 60 beats per minute) felt calmer, could study longer, and had a higher rate of retention as well as better grades according to their teachers.

These special music pieces, recorded at just the right tempo, activate the left and right brain for the maximum learning/retention effect. The music activates the right brain and the words the student is reading or saying aloud activates the left brain. This increases the learning potential a minimum of five times according to the research.

When your body hears the even, one beat per second of baroque music, your heart rate and pulse relax to the beat. When you are in this relaxed but alert state, your mind is able to concentrate more easily. Music corresponds to and affects our physiological conditions. During heavy mental work, our pulse and blood pressure rises, and it's usually more difficult to concentrate in this state. The baroque and Mozart music pieces on *The Mozart Effect* learning tapes and compact disks have been especially selected for their beat pattern, which reduces your blood pressure and pulse rate and increases your ability to learn at the same time.

Listen to these tapes when you study, work, or drive in the car to receive the tremendous benefits. This is the music of such composers as Mozart, Vivaldi, Pachelbel, Handel, and Bach. I use these tapes every day and find them to be extraordinarily effective. This is a simple way for you to gain a hidden advantage in the learning process.

A recent news article reported that researchers have discovered direct evidence that music stimulates different regions of the brain responsible for memory, motor control, timing and language. For the first time, researchers also have located specific areas of mental activity linked to emotional responses to music.

At McGill University in Montreal, neuroscientist Anne Blood, who conducted the study, said, "You can activate different parts of the brain, depending on what music you listen to. So music can stimulate parts of the brain that are under-active in neurological diseases or a variety of emotional disorders. Over time, we could retrain the brain in these disorders." Harvard University Medical School neurobiologist, Mark Jude Tramo, says that "undeniably, there is a biology of music. There is no question that there is specialization within the human brain for the processing of music. Music is biologically part of human life, just as music is aesthetically part of human life."

Based on all the available research, *Music for the Mozart Effect Volume III is* highly recommended in order to achieve the best results in learning, health and creativity.

The CDs are called *Music for the Mozart Effect, Volumes I, II and III.* Volume I is called Strengthen the Mind, Music for Intelligence & Learning (best used for studying). The suggested uses for how to listen are included with the CD's or tapes; Volume II - Heal the Body (best used for reducing stress, tension and accelerating healing); Volume III - Unlock the Creative Spirit - Music for Creativity & Imagination (best used during times you want to accelerate your creativity).

In addition, SiriusXM and internet radio have stations that plays nothing but Mozart. This is recommended as background music while studying and writing.

Chapter Six

READING TO REMEMBER

Books are, apart from the tireless effort and endless influence of a good teacher, the chief source of education, and through them you explore the richness of human experience and the wisdom of the ages. — William Armstrong

There is no such thing as an interesting book, there are only interested readers. — Ralph Waldo Emerson

Books are the carriers of civilization. Without books history is silent, literature dumb, science crippled, thought and speculation at a standstill. They are engines of change, windows on the world, lighthouses erected in the sea of time. — Barbara Tuchman

Whoever claims to be zealous of truth, of happiness, of wisdom or knowledge, aye even of the faith, must needs become a lover of books. — Richard de Bury

Generally, the skill of reading is *supposed to be* mastered at its most basic level in the second grade. It is the single most important skill in learning. The inability to read is the single greatest sociological indicator of juvenile delinquency later in life. Boys in particular will hide their inability to read until its cost in their learning ability is undeniable and the social cost in their lives enormous. In the United States, 14 percent of the population cannot read. This problem often begins in school and is subsequently hidden by schools. The 2013 National Assessment of Educational Progress (NAEP) reading test results demonstrate that far too many young people continue to read below grade level. Sixty-five percent of all US fourth graders scored "below proficient," which means that they are not reading at grade level. Only 35 percent of fourth graders are reading at or above grade level. In addition, 64 percent of eighth graders are reading below grade level, whereas 36 percent are reading at or above grade level. It appears that one's entire educational edifice and life trajectory is largely dependent on what one are required to master at age seven.

But even when one has mastered the basics of reading, few know how to read a book in a manner that enables them to remember what they are reading. Ironically, Mortimer Adler and Charles Van Doren have a four-hundred page book called *How to Read a Book: The Classic Guide to Intelligent Reading*. With the importance of reading to education and the failure of the US educational system in meeting this most basic educational standard, one might think that at some point students would be taught "how to read a book." Sadly, like so many other study skills, this is not the case.

We might start with a definition of reading by William Armstrong: "Reading is thinking. Reading consists of extracting, weighing, comparing, balancing, and applying to experience, thoughts from the printed page." Reading is not looking at a page!

Preparation for Reading

1. Get some exercise.

2. Find a regular solitary place.

3. Eliminate distractions.

4. Plan breaks (ten minutes per hour).

5. Sit at a desk with good lighting.

6. Listen to Mozart quietly in the background.

Kinds of Books

Books fall in roughly three different categories: popular, trade, and academic. Most popular bestsellers are written at an eighth grade level, which is also true of newspapers. This is the popular press. The trade press are semi-academic books, often on non-fiction subjects, that are written at a high-school or college level. Trade books may or may not have footnotes. And finally, there are university press books that are largely written for a college or graduate school audience and are subject to academic peer-review prior to publication. Extensive footnoting is expected. Consequently, they are the most academically credible. These are the kinds of books that are required for a professor to write in order to gain tenure. Many students gain information today from the internet and sources such as Wikipedia. A wiki is a hypertext publication collaboratively edited and managed by its own audience directly using a web browser. A typical wiki contains multiple pages for the subjects or scope of the project and may be either open to the public or limited to use within an organization for maintaining its internal knowledge base. It is not considered a reliable source for academic sourcing. Each level of book represents a different level of reading difficulty and academic credibility.

1. Popular – non-academic (junior high level, publisher example Simon & Schuster)

2. Trade – semi-academic (college level, publisher example Basic Books)

3. University Press – academic (graduate level, publisher example Oxford University Press)

Build a Personal Reference Library

To be a serious student, one must acquire a basic personal reference library. Some of this is mitigated by the growing availability of these open-source resources on the Internet. These reference tools might well include the following, depending on your interest and eventual academic college major.

1. Reference Tools
   - *The Shorter Oxford Dictionary* (33 percent of the twenty volume OED)
   - *The New Rand McNally College World Atlas*
   - *The Elements of Style*
   - *MLA Style Manual*
   - *Benét's Reader's Encyclopedia*
   - Louise Cowan and Os Guinness, *Invitation to the Classics*
   - *New King James Bible*
   - www.britannica.com

2. Devotional Classics (try to read once each year)
   - Augustine, *The Confessions*
   - Thomas á Kempis, *The Imitation of Christ*
   - Blaise Pascal, *Penseés*
   - John Bunyan, *The Pilgrim's Progress*

1. The Big Three Books to Master for an Educated Mind
   - Homer, *The Iliad* and *The Odyssey*
   - Fyodor Dostoevsky, *The Brothers Karamazov*
   - William Faulkner, *Go Down, Moses*

Reading for Growth

Reading is like a muscle: it gets stronger with practice and by reading more difficult material. On average Americans read for about seven minutes per day; 27 percent have not read a book in a year; and 74 percent read only one book per year. In spite of the growing number of books being published per year—three million new titles in 2011—the amount of serious reading being done by the average American is decreasing, obviously being replaced by television and social media. A serious student then needs to counter these patterns and make it a habit to read books.

"To stuff our minds with what is trivial, simply curious, or of a low nutritive power, is to close our minds to what is solid and enlarging, and spiritually sustaining." — Frederic Harrison

"If you are reading in order to become a better reader, you cannot read just any book or article. You will not improve as a reader if all you read are books that are well within your capacity. You must tackle books that are beyond you, or, as we have said, books that are over your head. Only books of that sort will make you stretch your mind. And unless you stretch, you will not learn." — Mortimer Adler

1. Improvement does not come with amusement.

2. Read to be stretched. Read progressively more difficult material.

3. Choose to read books worthy of the effort, the important books of influence within your field of study or calling.

4. Classics must be read more than once, to be truly appreciated. C.S. Lewis advises for every modern book you read, read one old one; or at least for every three modern, read one old book.

5. What ten books would you take with you on a desert island? Why?

6. Watch: Tracy Lee Simmons, "Great Books for Busy People: What the Best Books Teach Us Every Day," https://www.youtube.com/watch?v=HYKdJpwYuAo/.

How to Read a Book

Pre-Reading

1. Rephrase the title or the main heading into a question.

2. Examine all the subheadings, illustrations, and graphs in the chapter.

3. Read the introductory and summary paragraphs first.

4. Read the first sentence of every paragraph.

Reading

1. Read with a pen in hand prepared to underline the author's outline.

2. Write a list of the key terms or names (Who? When? Where? Why? How?)

3. Write a brief summary.

4. Answer four questions:
   • What is the main point?
   • What is the basic outline?
   • Is it true?
   • What is its significance?

Underlining

1. The goal of underlining is to reveal the author's outline. Most of the test questions will come from what has been underlined in your reading, often from the first or last sentence of the paragraph—this is particularly true of a

textbook. Ironically, most students are told not to mark their books, because they are not owned by the student. As a consequence, students are not taught to read to remember.

2. The purpose is to identify the main points and make it easier to understand.

3. The process of deciding what is important is the key to learning the material.

4. Underlining shortens the review process.

5. Avoid highlighters — this is coloring rather than learning. A person who predominately uses highlighters will rarely get better than a C average.

Analyzing

"Enlightenment is achieved only when, in addition to knowing what an author says, you know what he means and why he says it." — Mortimer Adler

1. Is there a clear message communicated throughout? It there a unifying metaphor or picture?

2. What is the author's perspective or point of view?

3. Is the author's argument objective or subjective, based on reality or opinion?

4. Are the arguments and conclusions consistent?

5. Are the explanations clear?

Summarizing

1. Write out test questions for the material.

2. Write out definitions to key terms. Numbers are not necessarily important unless they are tied to a key concept.

3. Reread the summary paragraph. If a textbook has a summary section, read it before and after you read the material assigned.

Remembering

1. You only remember what you understand.

2. You only remember what you choose to remember, which comes from "kneading" the information so as to put it into a memorable pattern.

3. You only remember if you go beyond the mere assignment. Reading is not looking at the assigned pages!

4. You only remember if you reorganize the material into a pattern. Learn with a pen in hand to take notes.

5. You only remember if you make associations with what you already know. Learning is a lot like LEGOs, you must connect the elements to one another.

Note Cards

1. Good check on rapid recall.

2. Put a page number on card for further reference.

3. Use mnemonics only when appropriate (For example, "*Red* touches black, safe for Jack. *Red* touches *yellow, kills a fellow.*" – a rhyme used to identify a king snake versus the poisonous coral snake)

4. Review at least weekly with a study partner or parent for approximately fifteen minutes.

Big Ideas
1. Reading to remember requires underlining.
2. Underline so as to reveal the author's outline.

Action Steps
1. Short-Term: Read "How to Mark a Book," which follows.

2. Long-Term: Purchase your textbooks so that you can underline them.

How To Mark A Book[1]

Mortimer J. Adler

You know you have to read "between the lines" to get the most out of anything. I want to persuade you to do something equally important in the course of your reading. I want to persuade you to write between the lines. Unless you do, you are not likely to do the most efficient kind of reading.

I contend, quite bluntly, that marking up a book is not an act mutilation but of love. You shouldn't mark up a book, which isn't yours.

Librarians (or your friends) who lend you books expect you to keep them clean, and you should. If you decide that I am right about the usefulness of marking books, you will have to buy them. Most of the world's great books are available today, in reprint editions.

There are two ways in which one can own a book. The first is the property right you establish by paying for it, just as you pay for clothes and furniture. But this act of purchase is only the prelude to possession. Full ownership comes only when you have made it a part of yourself, and the best way to make yourself a part of it is by writing in it. An illustration may make the point clear. You buy a beefsteak and transfer it from the butcher's icebox to your own. But you do not own the beefsteak in the most important sense until you consume it and get it into your bloodstream. I am

---

[1] Morimer Adler, "How to Mark a Book," *The Saturday Review of Literature*, July 6, 1941: https://stevenson.ucsc.edu/academics/stevenson-college-core-courses/how-to-mark-a-book-1.pdf.

arguing that books, too, must be absorbed in your bloodstream to do you any good.

Confusion about what it means to "own" a book leads people to a false reverence for paper, binding, and type—a respect for the physical thing—the craft of the printer rather than the genius of the author. They forget that it is possible for a man to acquire the idea, to possess the beauty, which a great book contains, without staking his claim by pasting his bookplate inside the cover. Having a fine library doesn't prove that is owner has a mind enriched by books; it proves nothing more than that he, his father, or his wife, was rich enough to buy them.

There are three kinds of book owners. The first has all the standard sets and best sellers—unread, untouched. (This deluded individual owns wood pulp and ink, not books.) The second has a great many books—a few of them read through, most of them dipped into, but all of them as clean and shiny as the day they were bought. (This person would probably like to make books his own but is restrained by a false respect for their physical appearance.) The third has a few books or many—every one of them dog-eared and dilapidated, shaken and loosened by continual use, marked and scribbled in from front to back. (This man owns books.)

Is it false respect, you may ask, to preserve intact and unblemished a beautifully printed book, an elegantly bound edition? Of course not. I'd no more scribble all over a first edition of *Paradise Lost* than I'd give my baby a set of crayons and an original Rembrandt. I wouldn't mark up a painting or a statue. Its soul, so to speak, is inseparable from its body. And the beauty of a rare edition or of a richly manufactured volume is like that of a painting or a statue.

But the soul of a book "can" be separate from its body. A book is more like the score of a piece of music than it is like a painting. No great musician confuses a symphony with the printed sheets of music. Arturo Toscanini reveres Brahms, but Toscanini's score of the G minor Symphony is so thoroughly marked up that no one but the maestro himself can read it. The reason why a great conductor makes notations on his musical scores—marks them up again and again each time he returns to study them—is the reason why you should mark your books. If your respect for magnificent binding or typography gets in the way, buy yourself a cheap edition and pay your respects to the author.

Why is marking up a book indispensable to reading? First, it keeps you awake. (And I don't mean merely conscious; I mean awake.) In the second place; reading, if it is active, is thinking, and thinking tends to express itself in words, spoken or written. The marked book is usually the thought-through book. Finally, writing helps you remember the thoughts you had, or the thoughts the author expressed. Let me develop these three points.

If reading is to accomplish anything more than passing time, it must be active. You can't let your eyes glide across the lines of a book and come up with an understanding of what you have read. Now an ordinary piece of light fiction, like, say, *Gone With the Wind*, doesn't require the most active kind of reading. The books you read for pleasure can be read in a state of relaxation, and nothing is lost. But a great book, rich in ideas and beauty, a book that raises and tries to answer great fundamental questions, demands the most active reading of which you are capable. You don't absorb the ideas of John Dewey the way you absorb the crooning of Mr. Vallee. You have reach for them. That you cannot do while you're asleep.

If, when you've finished reading a book, the pages are filled with your notes, you know that you read actively. The most famous "active" reader of great books I know is President Hutchins, of the University of Chicago. He also has the hardest schedule of business activities of any man I know. He invariably reads with a pencil, and sometimes, when he picks up a book and pencil in the evening, he finds himself, instead of making intelligent notes, drawing what he calls "caviar factories" on the margins. When that happens, he puts the book down. He knows he's too tired to read, and he's just wasting time.

But, you may ask, why is writing necessary? Well, the physical act of writing, with your own hand, brings words and sentences more sharply before your mind and preserves them better in your memory. To set down your reaction to important words and sentences you have read, and the questions they have raised in your mind, is to preserve those reactions and sharpen those questions.

Even if you wrote on a scratch pad and threw the paper away when you had finished writing, your grasp of the book would be surer. But you don't have to throw the paper away. The margins (top and bottom, and well as side), the end-papers, the very space between the lines, are all available. They aren't sacred. And, best of all, your marks and notes become an integral part of the book and stay there forever. You can pick up the book the following week or year, and there are all your points of agreement, disagreement, doubt, and inquiry. It's like resuming an interrupted conversation with the advantage of being able to pick up where you left off.

And that is exactly what reading a book should be: a conversation between you and the author. Presumably he knows more about the subject than you do; naturally, you'll have the proper humility as you approach him. But don't let anybody tell you that a reader is supposed to be solely on the receiving end. Understanding is a two-way operation; learning doesn't consist in being an empty receptacle. The learner has to question himself and question the teacher. He even has to argue with the teacher, once he understands what the teacher is saying. And marking a book is literally an expression of differences, or agreements of opinion, with the author.

There are all kinds of devices for marking a book intelligently and fruitfully. Here's the way I do it:

- **Underlining**: of major points, of important or forceful statements.

- **Vertical lines at the margin**: to emphasize a statement already underlined.

- **Star, asterisk, or other doo-dad at the margin**: to be used sparingly, to emphasize the ten or twenty most important statements in the book. (You may want to fold the bottom comer of each page on which you use such marks. It won't hurt the sturdy paper on which most modern books are printed, and you will be able take the book off the shelf at any time and, by opening it at the folded-corner page, refresh your recollection of the book.)

- **Numbers in the margin**: to indicate the sequence of points the author makes in developing a single argument.

- **Numbers of other pages in the margin**: to indicate where else in the book the author made points relevant to the point marked; to tie up the ideas in a book, which, though they may be separated by many pages, belong together.

- Circling or highlighting of key words or phrases.

- **Writing in the margin, or at the top or bottom of the page, for the sake of recording questions** (and perhaps answers) which a passage raised in your mind; reducing a complicated discussion to a simple statement; recording the sequence of major points right through the books. I use the end-papers at the back of the book to make a personal index of the author's points in the order of their appearance.

The front end-papers are to me the most important. Some people reserve them for a fancy bookplate. I reserve them for fancy thinking. After I have finished reading the book and making my personal index on the back end-papers, I turn to the front and try to outline the book, not page by page or point by point (I've already done that at the back), but as an integrated structure, with a basic unity and an order of parts. This outline is, to me, the measure of my understanding of the work.

If you're a die-hard anti-book-marker, you may object that the margins, the space between the lines, and the end-papers don't give you room enough. All right. How about using a scratch pad slightly smaller than the page-size of the book—so that the edges of the sheets won't protrude? Make your index, outlines and even your notes on the pad, and then insert these sheets permanently inside the front and back covers of the book.

Or, you may say that this business of marking books is going to slow up your reading. It probably will. That's one of the reasons for doing it. Most of us have been taken in by the notion that speed of reading is a measure of our intelligence. There is no such thing as the right speed for intelligent reading. Some things should be read quickly and effortlessly and some should be read slowly and even laboriously. The sign of intelligence in reading is the ability to read different things differently according to their worth. In the case of good books, the point is not to see how many of them you can get through, but rather how many can get through you—how many you can make your own. A few friends are better than a thousand acquaintances. If this be your aim, as it should be, you will not be impatient if it takes more time and effort to read a great book than it does a newspaper.

You may have one final objection to marking books. You can't lend them to your friends because nobody else can read them without being distracted by your notes. Furthermore, you won't want to lend them because a marked copy is kind of an intellectual diary, and lending it is almost like giving your mind away.

If your friend wishes to read your *Plutarch's Lives*, *Shakespeare*, or *The Federalist Papers*, tell him gently but firmly, to buy a copy. You will lend him your car or your coat—but your books are as much a part of you as your head or your heart.

Reading: The Decisive Variable

Reading, the most basic skill a student learns, is the foundation of all other academic pursuits.

Yet American students are notoriously weak readers: the United States ranks below Australia, England, Canada, Japan, France, and Russia in literacy. In the United States, approximately 35 to 40 percent of school-age children are below grade level in reading. More significantly, of the 40 percent who have difficulty with reading, approximately 80 percent are boys. Much of the fault lies with progressive whole-word methods of reading instruction (also called sight-reading or the immersion method). Recent brain research indicates why boys have difficulty learning to read using this approach.[2] Instead, reading instruction must be based on a thorough understanding of phonics.[3]

The vast number of students labeled as "learning different" or placed in "special education" tracks are the victims of defective teaching methods. If reading is difficult for a student, then all the

---

[2] Cliff Ponder, founder of Academic Associates, one of the premier reading instruction programs, writes, "Male and female brains, while similar in many respects, often function differently when processing the same or similar tasks. This is a result of physiological differences in the neural architecture of the brain over which neither the male nor female has any conscious control. These differences are graphically illustrated by magnetic resonance images taken during various activities.... The male in the 40 percent group is generally unable to draw abstract conclusions; and is thus unable to infer that letters are symbols that stand for sounds. He must be taught every possible sound represented by each letter and combination of letters, plus dependable rules that govern the sounds those letters make. Until he learns this, he will have difficulty reading." See www.academic-associates.com/the_problem.htm, Sally Shaywitz, "Dyslexia," *Scientific American*, (November 1996), and Marilyn Jager Adams's *Beginning to Read: Thinking and Learning About Print*.

[3] Ponder writes, "Although many reading programs have been devised, with sophisticated-sounding names that promise to teach reading without learning the sounds and the rules that govern them, the only method that works consistently is a comprehensive, systematic approach to phonics." For a more detailed discussion on the importance of reading in closing the education gap see E.D. Hirsch's *The Knowledge Deficit: Closing the Shocking Education Gap for American Children.*

rest of school will be difficult. In fact, illiteracy is the single most determinative variable in juvenile delinquency.

In most schools, reading instruction is completed by the second grade and often only one reading instruction specialist will assist in teaching reading. Thus, either seven-year-old students get it or they don't, and are moved on to an uncertain future. This problem occurs year to year despite the fact that a student's educational success and personal confidence depends on this one skill alone. Compounding poor reading instruction is the demise of reading itself in a visually oriented culture, since books are no longer esteemed in a culture dominated by TV, video games, and computers.[4] Ken Myers suggests the significance of the problem for Christians: "A culture that is rooted more in images than in words will find it increasingly difficult to sustain *any* broad commitment to truth, since truth is an abstraction requiring language." The development of a Christian mind begins then with a thorough grasp of phonics, grammar, and vocabulary. Teachers and students in a Christian school as well as homeschooling parents should honor words, reading, and books as the enculturation of language. Cambridge University philosopher George Steiner writes,

> The complex of the book and of its reader stands in a specific Judaic-Hellenic descent. It is from these two antique sources, so oddly, so intensely literary and bookish in their self-definition, that we derive our view of the eminent worth and stability of speech. These two civilizations tell us that the word—the *logos*—is central to man's religion, to his *log*ic, to his mytho*log*ies.

---

[4] See Douglas Groothius's appendix, "Television: Agent of Truth Decay," in *Truth Decay: Defending Christianity Against the Challenges of Postmodernity*. Steiner laments, "A large majority of those who pass through the primary and secondary school system can 'read' but not *read*. Theirs is a pseudo-literacy."

The phrase "People of the Book", coined by Muhammad, the Prophet of Islam, distinguished the religious culture based on a revelation handed down orally versus one handed down in writing, and it was first attached to the Jews as a pejorative description. We gladly embrace the label. For Christians, reading must be seen as a spiritual discipline. God gave us a book, not a video.

Chapter Seven

MEMORIZING FACTS

We remember what we understand; we understand only what we pay attention to; we pay attention to what we want. — Edward Bolles

Memorization has gotten a bad rap recently. Lots of students, and even some educators, say that being able to reason is more important than knowing facts; and besides, why bother committing things to memory when you've got Google? My response to this—after I've finished inwardly groaning—is that of course reasoning is important, but that doesn't mean you shouldn't know facts as well. It's not like you have to choose between one or the other. Besides, facts give you a foundation on which to reason about things.
— Stefanie Weisman

God's Word must be so strongly fixed in our minds that it becomes the dominant influence in our thoughts, our attitudes, and our actions. One of the most effective ways of influencing our minds is through memorizing Scripture. David said, 'I have hidden Your Word in my heart that I might not sin against You' (Psalm 119:11).
—Jerry Bridges

Memorization is not opposed to thinking but instead provides the building blocks *for* thinking. Moreover, if the brain is like a muscle, then memorization is like working out with weights. It strengthens the mind so that you have greater facility in doing other "athletic" mental activities.

1. *Change the way you use your memory.* Memory itself probably cannot be developed; however, improvement in remembering comes from correcting certain habits or thoughts so that we use our memory to its fullest potential. Remembering is like seeing; improvement in either function does not depend upon how much we use it but, rather, how we use it.

2. *Pay close attention.* The first and most important rule for remembering is: cultivate the habit of close attention to the thing you wish to remember. Be sure you have a clear, sharp impression of the face, name, date, or facts that you will need to know at a future time. If you wish to remember a fact, make it meaningful. If you are interested in a boy or a girl, you will easily memorize their phone number.

3. *Get your senses involved.* When we are learning, we should try not only to get a strong impression but obtain as many different kinds of impressions as possible. Some people can remember colors distinctly but have a poor memory for shapes. But anyone, by putting together and using all of the impressions our sense organs bring us about a thing, can remember it much more clearly than if we rely on sight or sound alone. For example, try rereading your lesson aloud. In doing this, your eye takes in the appearance of the printed word, your ear passes the sound of the words to your brain, and even the tension of the muscles of your throat adds their bit to that total impression, which your mind is expected to store away.

4. *Try to visualize it.* Either remember a diagram or a picture of the material to be remembered, or take short notes about it, which you can visualize.

5. *Intend to remember.* The mere intention to remember puts the mind in a condition to remember, and if you will make use of this fact in studying you will be able to recall between 20 percent and 60 percent more of what you read and hear than you would if you were not actively trying to remember.

6. *Think about it.* A fact doesn't belong to you until you have used it. In making use of this principle, plan to spend no more than one-half of your study period in reading your lesson. *Use the other half in doing something with what you learn.* Think about what you have studied, write down notes on it, and explain it to somebody else. To learn something well, teach it!

7. *Use your logical memory.* An important aid to the remembering process is the habit of associating a new idea immediately with facts or ideas that are already firmly lodged in your mind. This association revives and strengthens the old memories and prevents the new one from slipping away by anchoring it to the well-established framework of your mental world.

8. *Remember by brute force.* We will forget more, on the average, during the first hour after learning than during the next twenty-four hours; and we will forget more on the average, during the first day than we will during the next thirty days. Whatever is left *after thirty days*, we will probably be able to hold on to without much further loss for years to come. *Remember something for thirty days and you will have learned it for life.*

9. *Review consistently.* Reviewing is much more effective if carried out before memories have entirely escaped than it

is after considerable time has elapsed. Repetitions should be strung out over as long a time as is available. We remember better if we pause a little between periods of study. Re-learning something forgotten is not reviewing.

10. *Study 50 percent more.* How much study do you need? You should study more than enough to learn your assignment. Experiments have proven that 50 percent more resulted in 50 percent better retention. After a week had passed, it was found that extra work had salvaged six times as much of the material as in the case when it was barely learned.

11. *Short study sessions are your friend.* Learning advances more quickly in *many short sessions* than it does in a few long ones. This is especially true of definitions, lists, and vocabulary. This means that reviewing is mostly about consistent time management.

12. *Test yourself.* Testing yourself has a far greater impact than simply reviewing. Testing focuses your attention on specific elements (areas of ignorance), turning a passive review into a motivated search for answers.

Big Idea
1. Memorization happens best in short, repeated sessions.
2. If something is learned for thirty days, it can be remembered for life.
3. Every field or course has facts that must be memorized. Memorize them early.

Action Steps

1. Short-Term: For each course write up a basic fact sheet to be memorized: dates, definitions, formulas, equations, poems, and the like.

2. Long-Term: Commit the fact sheets to memory over the course of the first semester.

Memory and Related Learning Principles[5]

The Principles of Short-Term and Long-Term Memory

The principle of long-term memory may well be at work when you *recite* or *write* the ideas and facts that you read. As you recite or write you are holding each idea in mind for the four or five seconds that are needed for the temporary memory to be converted into a permanent one. In other words, the few minutes that it takes for you to review and think about what you are trying to learn is the minimum length of time that neuroscientists believe is necessary to allow thought to go into a lasting, more easily retrievable memory.

Recognition is an easier stage of memory than the *recall* stage. For example, in an examination, it is much easier to *recognize* an answer to a question if five options are listed, than to *recall* the answer without the options listed. But getting beyond just recognizing the correct answer when you see it is usually necessary for long-term memory, for the more we can recall about information the better we usually remember it.

Understanding New Material

First and most important, you must make sure that you understand new material before trying to remember it. A good technique to ensure understanding is to recite or write the author's ideas in your *own words*. If you cannot, then you do not understand them. The conclusion: you cannot remember what you do not understand. In other words, you cannot form a clear

---

[5] http://web-us.com/memory/memory_and_related_learning_prin.htm/.

93

and correct memory trace from a fuzzy, poorly understood concept.

In the classroom, do not hesitate to ask the instructor to explain further a point that is not clear to you. If the point is unclear to you, there is a good chance that it is unclear to others, so you will not be wasting anyone's time. Furthermore, most instructors appreciate the opportunity to answer questions.

Getting It Right the First Time

We have learned that all remembering depends on forming an original, clear neural trace in the brain in the first place. These initial impressions are vitally important because the mind clings just as tenaciously to incorrect impressions as it does to correct impressions. Then we have to unlearn and relearn. Incorrect information is so widespread that Mark Twain once wrote, "Education consists mainly in what we have unlearned."

Evaluate the Learning

Evaluate the Learning. Another way to improve retention is through evaluation. After you have studied, work the matter over in your mind. Examine and analyze it; become familiar with it like a friend. Use comparison or contrast: How is this topic like or different from related topics? If the learning concerns things conjectural, do you tend to agree or disagree? Are there aspects of the subject that you can criticize? Analytical thinking encourages you to consider the matter from various aspects and this kind of mental manipulation makes you more knowledgeable. For all these reasons, recall is significantly improved.

The Principle of Over-learning

After you have recited a lesson long enough to say it perfectly, if you continue reciting it a few times more, you will over-learn it. A well-known psychologist and researcher, Ebbinghaus, has reported that each additional recitation (after you really know the material) engraves the mental trace deeper and deeper, thus establishing a base for long-term retention. For many people over learning is difficult to practice because, by the time they achieve bare mastery, there is little time left and they are eager to drop the subject and go on to something else. But reciting the material even just one more time significantly increases retention, so try to remember this and utilize the technique when you can.

The Principle of Recitation
There is no principle that is more important or more effective than *recitation* for transferring material from the short-term memory to the long-term memory. For one thing, you are obviously in the process of repeating the information. Recitation can take several forms—thinking about it, writing it out, or saying it out loud. "Thinking about it" is potentially the least effective because it gives us the least amount of reinforcement since writing or speaking involve more electrical muscle movement messages to the brain which are known to increase mental response and recording. Vocal, "out loud" recitation is usually the most effective single technique for review because it employs more of the senses than any other review technique (utilizing both auditory and vocal senses). If, for example, when reviewing your notes immediately after class the reviewing is done by vocal recitation, you will not only be consolidating the new information but also strengthening the neural traces made to your brain.

What Is Recitation?
Recitation is simply saying aloud the ideas that you want to remember. For example, after you have gathered your information in note form and have categorized and clustered your items, you recite them. Here's how: you cover your notes, and then recite aloud the covered material. After reciting, expose the notes and check for accuracy. You should not attempt to recite the material word for word; rather your reciting should be in the words and manner that you would ordinarily use if you were explaining the

material to a friend. When you can *say* it, then you know it. (This is why it is best *not* to recite directly from the text.)

How Recitation Works

Recitation transfers material to the secondary or long-term memory. While you are reading the words in a sentence or paragraph, the *primary memory* (short-term memory) holds them in mind long enough for you to gain the sense of the sentence or paragraph. However, the primary memory has a very limited capacity, and as you continue to read, you displace the words and ideas of the initial paragraphs with the words of subsequent paragraphs. This is one reason for not remembering everything in the first part of the chapter by the time we reach the end of the chapter when we read continually without taking a break or taking time to review what we have already read.

It is only when we *recite* or contemplate the idea conveyed by a sentence or paragraph that the idea has a chance (not guaranteed) of moving on into the *secondary memory* (a long-term storage facility).

All verbal information goes first into the primary memory (short-term memory). When it is rehearsed (recited), part of it goes into our secondary (long-term) memory. The rest of it, usually the part we are least interested in, returns to the primary memory and is then forgotten.

Whether new information is "stored" or "dumped" depends, then, on our reciting it out loud and on our interest in the information.

After seven days the amount remembered by students who did no review was 33 percent and those who reviewed was 83 percent. After sixty-three days, the amount of material remembered by students who did not review was 14 percent versus 70 percent by those who reviewed.

Remembering

As a student, one of your main concerns is to retain old learnings while you continue to acquire new ones. Do we remember more when we begin to study a subject or after we already know something about it? According to several recent studies, learning that involves memorization of a unit of material begins slowly, then goes faster, and finally levels off. In other words, the amount learned per unit of time is small at first, then increases, and then becomes small again. This finding contrasts with older studies, which showed that learning was rapid at first, then became slower until it leveled off.

Even though a person continues to study, he may expect to encounter periods when there seems to be little or no gain. Such *plateaus* in learning may be due to several causes such as fatigue, loss of interest, or diminishing returns from using the same inefficient methods. Another explanation of plateaus is that they represent *pauses* between stages of understanding; when the student acquires a new insight, he can move on. Sometimes the lower stage of an understanding or a skill may actually *interfere* with progress to a higher level. For example, learning to read by individual letters of the alphabet interferes with learning to read by words. Learning to read word-by-word delays reading by phrases or sentences.

The important thing is to recognize that plateaus or periods of slow learning are inevitable, and they should not discourage the student unduly. Learning may still be taking place, but at a slower pace. Recognizing that he is at a plateau, the student should first try to analyze and improve his study methods, if possible. Sometimes, however, an incorrect mental set may be interfering with the necessary perception of new relationships. Sometimes slow learning may simply be due to fatigue. In either of these circumstances the most efficient procedure may be to drop the activity temporarily and return to it later, after a good night's rest.

The rate at which a student learns depends upon his learning ability, but slow learners remember just as well as fast learners, provided that they have learned the material equally well. The reason a bright student may do better on examinations is that he has learned the subject matter more effectively within the time available. But if a slower student spends enough time on his studies, he can retain every bit as much as the faster student. Fortunately, there is evidence that both rate of learning and rate of retention can be improved with practice.

The Principle of Neuro-Transmitter Depletion

Often students study or attempt to read for too long a period of time without stopping for a rest break. B.F. Skinner and other experts have concluded that the average student cannot usually study really difficult material efficiently for more than about four hours a day. Then efficiency and memory begin to suffer. Research shows that the average student cannot study effectively on the same subject for more than about four consecutive hours, even with short breaks every hour. What occurs is what is referred to as the principle of neuro-transmitter depletion. Neuroscientists have developed techniques to monitor activity (usually defined as electrical impulses) and chemical changes in the brain during study or thought processing. If one studies the same subject too long, fatigue, boredom, and sometimes slight disorientation may occur. It is a common result of too much consecutive study when even the simplest concept begins not to make sense any longer. The monitoring of brain activity and chemical changes indicate that studying too long results in a depletion of chemicals in the brain cells necessary for efficient processing of information. *Therefore, for effective consolidation of material into memory storage, take frequent breaks (at least ten minutes every hour) and do not attempt to deal with really difficult material for more than about four hours a day, and do not study any easier subject area (even with breaks) for more than four consecutive hours.*

SAMPLE KEY DATES SHEET

Western Civilization II

You cannot meaningfully be a student of history if you are unclear about the major themes and events of particular centuries. Therefore, when I taught AP European History, students were required to memorize these dates and chronological sequences.

The same principle is true of every academic discipline, there is a basic sequence of facts to be memorized. Memorize these fact sheets for the course early.

The Hierarchy of Christendom

Early Middle Age (900–1000)

High Middle Age (1000–1300)

Disintegration (1300–1400)

9th Century   Celtic and Carolingian Renaissance

10th Century   Invasions

11th Century   Feudalism

12th Century   Papacy and Crusades

13th Century   Scholasticism

14th Century   Disintegration
- Avignon Papacy 1305–1376
- The Hundred Years' War 1337–1453

- Black Death 1350–1450
- The Great Schism 1378–1417

15th Century   Renaissance (Italy and Portugal dominant)
- Fall of Constantinople 1453
- Medici in Florence 1434–1492
- Columbus 1492
- Leonardo da Vinci 1452–1519

16th Century   Reformations (Spain dominant)
- Desiderius Erasmus 1466–1536
- Martin Luther's 95 Theses 1517
- John Calvin's *Institutes* 1536
- Thomas More 1478–1535
- Ignatius of Loyola 1491–1556
- Peace of Augsburg 1555 (*"cuius regio eius religio"*)
- Wars of Religion 1562–1598
- Defeat of the Spanish Armada 1588

17th Century   Science (Dutch dominant)
- East India Company 1602
- Bank of Amsterdam 1609
- Francis Bacon's *Novum Organum* 1620
- René Descartes' *Discourse on Method* 1637
- Isaac Newton's *Principia* 1687
- Peace of Westphalia 1648
- Regicide of Charles I 1649
- Glorious Revolution 1688
- Absolutism of Louis XIV 1643–1715

18th Century   Enlightenment (France dominant)
- Peter the Great 1682–1725
- The "Bubbles" 1720
- John Wesley 1703–1791
- Denis Diderot's *Encyclopédie* 1772

- Jean-Jacque Rousseau's *Social Contract* 1762
- The French Revolution 1789
- Napoleon's "Republic" 1792–1814
- Congress of Vienna 1815

19th Century   Industrialism and Nationalism (England dominant)
- Karl Marx's *Communist Manifesto* 1848
- European Revolutions 1848
- American Civil War 1860–1865
- Nationalism 1859–1871
- Imperialism 1875–1914
- Charles Darwin's *Origins of the Species* 1859
- Sigmund Freud's *Interpretation of Dreams* 1900
- Friedrich Nietzsche 1844–1900

20th Century   Totalitarianism (United States dominant)
- Battle of Mukden 1904
- World War I 1914–1918
- Treaty of Versailles 1919
- Bolshevik Revolution 1917
- The Crash of 1929
- The Nazi State 1933–1945
- World War II 1940–1945
- United Nation's *Declaration of Human Rights* 1948
- Vietnam War 1960–1971
- Collapse of Communism 1989

Chapter Eight

SECRETS OF WRITING PAPERS

Do not say a little in many words, but a great deal in a few.
— Pythagoras

To a beginner, the advice I would give would be to think straight and write simply. To be clear is the first duty of a writer; to charm and to please are graces to be acquired later.
— Brander Matthews

Vigorous writing is concise. A sentence should contain no unnecessary words, a paragraph no unnecessary sentences, for the same reason that a drawing should have no unnecessary lines and a machine no unnecessary parts.
— William Strunk, Jr.

There are two kinds of writing that make up a basic student's experience: the three-paragraph essay and the research paper. The three-paragraph essay is typically used in essay exams, while research papers are usually assigned late in your high school experience. Both are critically important skills to master. And behind this skill is the skill of outlining. It should be clear from what follows that in most schools today good writing skills are not taught.

Basic Essay

The basic three-paragraph essay is composed of a thesis paragraph, an evidence paragraph and a conclusion (in other words, an introduction, body, and conclusion). The introduction should start with a hook to gain the readers interest, perhaps a picture or compelling metaphor. It should also take a position on a given thesis. The body of the essay provides evidence for the thesis in descending strength—giving the strongest evidence first. And finally, the conclusion should summarize the thesis and suggest its implications and restate the overarching picture or metaphor. The three-paragraph essay is the opposite of creative writing. It follows a strict formula.

Taking an Essay Test

Learn the meanings of the important directive words that appear in an essay question. For students to write effective answers to essay questions, they must understand clearly the meanings of words, such as the following, that tell them how to present the material. A good essay closely follows the directions. The essay question tells you how to organize your material. Examples here are from European history exams.

- **Analyze.** Determine their component parts; examine their nature and relationship. "Analyze the social and technological changes that took place in European warfare between 1789 and 1871."

- **Assess/Evaluate.** Judge the value or character of something; appraise; evaluate the positive points and the negative ones; give an opinion regarding the value of; discuss the advantages and disadvantages of. "'Luther was both a revolutionary and a conservative.' Evaluate this statement with respect to Luther's responses to the political and social questions of his day."

- **Compare.** Examine for the purpose of noting similarities and differences. "Compare the rise of power of fascism in Italy and Germany."

- **Contrast.** Examine in order to show dissimilarities or points of difference. "Contrast the ways in which European skilled artisans of the mid-eighteenth century and European factory workers of the late nineteenth century differed in their work behavior and in their attitudes toward work."

- **Describe.** Give an account of; tell about; give a word picture of. "Describe the steps taken between 1832 and 1918 to extend the suffrage in England. What groups and what movements contributed to the extension of the vote?"

- **Discuss.** Talk over; write about; consider or examine by argument or from various points of view; debate; present different sides of. "Discuss the extent to which nineteenth-century Romanticism was or was not a conservative cultural and intellectual movement."

- **Explain.** Make clear or plain; make clear the causes or reasons for; make known in detail; tell the meaning of. "Explain how economic, political, and religious factors promoted explorations from about 1450 to about 1525."

Most common errors:
- Simply paraphrasing or summarizing the question
- Failure to answer the question that is being asked *in the manner being asked*
- Failure to take a position or articulate a thesis
- Failure to give evidence for a position
- Failure to have a coherent argument
- Failure to show implications of the thesis

Make sure that you know how to do what is asked in the question.
- Read the directions and the question carefully.
- Try to evaluate the points of view of the sources and authors referenced.
- Demonstrate critical judgment—as in a trial lawyer before a jury.

Practice and training in writing essay responses can be done on a regular basis, both as part of a homework assignment and as a classroom exercise. In class, working under the time pressure of a mock exam situation helps students learn to resist the temptation to write before thinking. It also trains students to organize their thoughts, to answer the question directly, and to use a logical, structured thought process.

Failure of Teaching Writing
Writing is not taught well in most contemporary schools. Therefore, it is necessary for students to take up the task of learning this study skill themselves.

[An Aside for English Teachers
The proponents of expressive self-discovery have overtaken writing instruction like so many other aspects of the contemporary curriculum. The rigorous rules of grammar, syntax, and usage have long been abandoned. Hillsdale journalism professor Tracy Simmons writes, "For over the previous 20 years the academic instruction of writing in America has been transformed from an apprenticeship in careful utterance—burdened with grammar and rules of usage and endless red-pencil-marked themes—to a smooth path to an easy grade. Everybody can do it. Just open the dikes of the repressed psyche and watch the creative tide flow to the broad, calm waters of mental and emotional health." An essay is less about giving your subjective opinion about a subject as giving evidence for a thesis.

Robert Einarsson adds, "Composition classes involve paragraphs, essays, and creative writing, but not the basic building block of expression, sentences. Students today receive little or no instruction in sentence structure and grammar, a situation that was unthinkable fifty years ago. For some thousands of years and more, grammar was the mainstay of intellectual education; but, on the authority of a handful of education experts today, it has now been all but deleted from the English curriculum."

Will Fitzhugh, editor of *The Concord Review*, laments the loss of the high school term paper. "It seems likely that the history research paper at the high school level is now an endangered species. A focus on creative writing, fear of plagiarism, fascination with PowerPoint presentations, and a lack of time to meet with the students to plan papers (and to read them carefully when they are turned in) are factors in its decline." Research papers take far more effort for the teacher to grade well than other kinds of evaluation. In such disrepair is writing instruction that few teachers even know where to begin.

Schools that emphasize rhetoric in the upper grades—such as most classically-oriented schools—have an advantage. "Rhetoric is the craft of setting down words and marks right; or again: Rhetoric shows you how to put words together so that the reader not simply may but must grasp your meaning." Simmons suggests that good writing must be taught prescriptively. He writes, "Grammar and usage together, not self-expression, should be the lodestar for the writing course." Books such as Jacque Barzun's *Simple & Direct: A Rhetoric for Writers* and Scott Crider's *The Office of Assertion: An Art of Rhetoric for the Academic Essay* should be incorporated into the writing curriculum.

We must once again capture a respect for the power of words. Aleksandr Solzhenitsyn spoke of words as weapons—just as a shout in the mountains has been known to cause an avalanche, so words rightly placed can bring down nations: "Books are like divisions or army corps: at times they must dig themselves in, hold their fire, lie low; at times they just cross bridges in the dark and noiselessly; at times, concealing their preparations to the last dribble of loose earth, they must rush into a concerted offensive from the least expected quarter at the least expected moment. While the author is like a commander-in-chief, here throwing in a unit, there moving up another to wait its turn."

Richard Weaver adds, "The sentence through its office of assertion is a force adding itself to the forces of the world, and therefore the man clever with his sentences... was regarded with that uneasiness we feel in the presence of power." Crider, basing his approach to writing instruction on classical rhetoric, teaches writing in three stages: *invention*—what you say; *organization*—in what order you state your argument; and *style*—how you state your argument. Since writing is hard work, writing instruction is an arduous task.

One of the best approaches to writing instruction is "writing by imitation"—learning the art of writing from the writings of master wordsmiths. This is the approach taken in Francine Prose's *Reading Like a Writer: A Guide for People Who Love Books and for Those Who Want to Write Them*. She writes, "Skimming just won't suffice if we hope to extract one fraction of what a writer's words can teach us about how to use the language. And reading quickly—for plot, for ideas, even for the psychological truths that a story reveals—can be a hindrance when the crucial revelations are in the spaces between words, in what has been left out." In this method, less is more, close reading more important than expansive reading.

First students master sentences, then paragraphs, and finally essays. They master identification of clauses and phrases and the four types of sentences. When writing paragraphs, they learn to distinguish between the four modes of writing: *narration, description, exposition,* and *argumentation.* They take a sentence or paragraph from a master and analyze its structure and composition. What is the topic sentence? Write the subject and predicate of the topic sentence. What is the total number of sentences in the paragraph? Count the number of simple sentences. Count the number of compound sentences. Count the number of complex sentences. Count the number of compound/complex sentences. List any noteworthy grammatical construction. Then and only then do they write an imitation of the sample paragraph following closely the same grammatical and sentence structure. Here is an example of a paragraph students might profitably analyze and imitate from Thomas Flexner's *Washington: The Indispensable Man*:

> Although no one had yet recognized the fact, Hamilton and Jefferson were born to hate each other. Alike in having dominant personalities, they were opposite in manners and temperament. A shorter man than Jefferson, Hamilton moved with military crispness; Jefferson slouched. Hamilton dressed meticulously; even Jefferson's admirers felt he overdid the sloppiness of a philosopher. Hamilton's mind moved in the straight line of a doer; Jefferson's with the discursiveness of a thinker.]

Essay Writing
By first learning how words work in sentences and sentences in paragraphs students can learn to write well. Mastering the

paragraph using the paragraphs of masters is the key. Only then should students be allowed to write their own essays.

When writing their essays, students should approach them rhetorically, breaking down the project initially into the three steps of invention, organization, and style. In this way, students learn that all good writing begins with thinking and ends with countless revisions and polishing. Here are the three steps to writing an essay:

Invention: what you say
- Assignment: the occasion for your writing
- Focus: the degree to which what you say remains relevant to the occasion
- Argument: the main stance or position concerning what you say
- Development/Logic: how well what you say is explained
- Evidence: the facts/opinions that effectively support your position

Organization: in what order you state your argument
- Introduction: how you begin
  1) Informing your audience
  2) Disposing your audience to be receptive

- Body: presentation of logic and proof for your position
  1) Narratio: statement of fact about your subject
  2) Confirmatio: proof for your position
  3) Refutatio: refutation of opposing views

- Conclusion: how you end
  1) Inspire
  2) Amplify
  3) Rouse emotion
  4) Summarize argument and master metaphor

- Paragraphing: the division of your proof into discrete sections

- Transitions: the movement from one paragraph to another

Style: how you state your argument
- Variation: the different sentence structures you employ to express your ideas

- Grammar: the degree to which you follow the conventional rules of English usage

- Punctuation: the degree to which you follow the proper use of punctuation

- Diction: the different words you employ to express your ideas

- Citation: the formatting of your work according to appropriate or assigned guidelines

A student should not be allowed to sit at a computer and write an essay off the top of his or her head the night before it is due. This bad habit is encouraged by not first breaking the writing process down into its component steps, giving a concrete example of what is expected, and mastering each step sequentially. Ideally, homework should encourage the student to take these three steps. Like successful instruction of reading and mathematics, this systematic approach based on following rules and modeling the masters is the surest way to make writing one's own and subsequently finding one's own voice. Voice follows imitation just as creativity follows discipline. "While learning to write well can be satisfying," Simmons warns, "it isn't fun. Don't tell anyone it is." Good writing is hard work as it is also evidence of good thinking.

General Writing Guidelines

1. Most Important Skill
   - Thesis – a one-sentence summary of an argument.
   - Outline – a detailed blueprint of an argument

2. Three Steps to Writing
   - Invention – discovering the argument
   - Organization – designing the argument
   - Style – polishing the argument

3. Thesis

   - Prepare before writing
     - Purpose
     - Audience
     - Thesis or research question and point-of-view

   - What is the topic?

   - What are you asserting?

   - Is the assertion true?

   - What are the counter-arguments?

   - Summary
     - Is it a complete sentence?
     - Is every word clear and unambiguous in meaning?
     - Is the sentence a dead-end or does it call for additional information and explanation?
     - Does the statement make such a large claim that you have no hope of proving it to be true short of writing a book?

- What evidence is needed before someone will believe this thesis?

4. Outline (one of the most important study skills)
   - Benefit
     - Helps organize ideas (be cautious of outlining software as it does too much of the "kneading" for you and minimizes the benefits of the process)
     - Presents material in a logical form
     - Shows relationships among ideas in the argument
     - Provides an overview
     - Establishes boundaries
     - Prevents writer's block
     - Process aids memorization
     - Balances argument
     - Defines research directions

   - Uses
     - Reading
     - Studying
     - Speaking
     - Writing
     - Meetings
     - Conferences
     - Web Design
     - Project Management
     - Time Management

   - Process
     - Verbal
     - Graphic or Brainstorming
     - Linear

- Errors (informational vs. instructional)
  - Too thin (particularly for a writing aid)
  - Too detailed (particularly for a study aid)

- Theory
  - **Parallelism**–coordinate heads should be expressed in parallel **form** (nouns with nouns, verbs with verbs)

  - **Coordination**–items of equal significance have **comparable** numerical or letter designation (like with like)

  - **Subordination**–organize **logically** from general to specific or from abstract to concrete or past to present and same relationship should be maintained

  - **Division**–each section must always have at least two parts and basis of division needs to be sharp and of a similar kind

  - **Form**–consistency is the most important rule (brief and typed is best)

    An outline can use Roman numerals/letters or decimal form.

Roman Numeral Form

I.

    A.

    B.

        1.

        2.

            a.

            b.

                1)

                2)

Decimal Form (common in legal documents)

1.0

   1.1

   1.2

      1.2.1

      1.2.2

         1.2.2.1

         1.2.2.2

- Study Aid
  - Organize all of the exam material into 2–3 typed sheets of paper
  - Define the key terms, summarize the main ideas and show how they relate to each other

Research Paper

A research paper is an extended essay in which you explain what you have learned after exploring your topic in depth. In a research paper, you include information from sources such as books, articles, interviews, and Internet sites. You also use your own ideas, knowledge, and opinions to draw specific conclusions.

1. A research paper assumes that you have done research, namely read widely on the topic and explored alternative points of view on it. Two-thirds of the time taken on a research paper should be in research preparation. You cannot just sit down and write a research paper without

taking the time to do research. This is the cause of most forms of plagiarism.

2. A research paper draws on various sources as evidence. All of these sources need to be given adequate sourcing and documentation in footnotes. Ideally, these sources need to have academic credibility meaning that they are from trade or university press books and journals. When at all possible avoid general internet sources, unless they are providing open sources for academic journal articles.

3. As you prepare your research material, type up potential quotes with page citations from every book or source cited. For example,

Research Topic

Bibliographic Information about book or source

Quotes with page number at the end of each quote (2)

Bold the quotes you really like

4. Develop a typed bibliography and quote sheet

5. Develop a detailed outline

6. Cut and paste the relevant quotes into the outline

7. Write paper while keeping track of your citations carefully as you write (avoid having to find quotes after the fact, which is a waste of time, and happens all the time)

8. Avoid quoting too much from any one source. A short research paper should use three to six sources.

9. Maintain balance and remember to focus on your thesis. Don't lose track of what you are trying to prove or demonstrate with the paper. Tie each paragraph back to the thesis.

10. Work on a bibliography, which is a listing of all the sources you referred to in preparation for writing this thesis, particularly those not used in direct citations. This is a broader list of sources. Footnotes are the sources used in the paper, and the bibliography is composed of the sources used in preparation for writing the paper, that is the general research conducted before writing.

11. Revise, revise, revise

12. Plagiarism
    *   Plagiarism is a major violation of the academic code of ethics.
    *   Plagiarism is a combination of stealing and lying.
    *   One plagiarism violation on your academic record can keep you from getting into college. Avoid it. Teachers can always tell a plagiarized paper!
    *   If you have questions about your work, ask.
    *   Internet-based plagiarism is the most common form of plagiarism—copying or buying papers on given topics. All good teachers can spot a bought paper! A signed copy of the school's academic pledge should be attached to the paper.

        "I pledge before God and the school community that this work reflects my own intellectual effort and that no unauthorized help has been given or received."

Big Ideas
1. Basic essay and research paper writing is writing according to a formula. It is not creative writing.
2. Master the short essay before attempting a research paper.
3. Two-thirds of the time spent on a research paper should be spent on research—probably a minimum of ten hours for a five-page paper.

Action Steps
1. Short-Term: Write out a sample essay question prior to taking a test.

2. Long-Term: Ask your teacher for a copy of an excellent research paper as a guide for your writing.

SAMPLE OUTLINE

Purpose: To show how programs written for microcomputers relate to the process of writing.

Thesis: Microcomputer programs can have a positive effect on students' writing if both the potentials and limitations of the programs are understood.

Audience: Junior and high school students.

Microcomputer Programs and the Process of Writing

I. Major Steps in the Writing Process

    A. Organizing

    B. Writing the first draft

    C. Evaluating

    D. Revising

II. Writing Programs for the Microcomputer

    A. Types of Programs and Their Relationship to the Writing Process

        1. Thought
          a. Use in organizing
          b. Use in revising

2. Word Processors
   a. Use in writing the first draft
   b. Use in revising

3. Analytical programs: grammar, style, and spelling
   a. Use in evaluating
   b. Use in revising

B. Positive and Negative Aspects of Computer Writing Programs

   1. Positive features
      a. Less time spent on repetitive or mechanical writing tasks
      b. Greater flexibility and versatility in writing process
      c. Increased revision strategies
      d. Specific learning possibilities

   2. Negative features
      a. The increased time spent on learning software programs and computers
      b. The availability of hardware and software
      c. The unrealistic expectations of users
         1) A cure-all for writing problems
         2) A way to avoid learning correct grammar/syntax/spelling
         3) A method to reduce time spent on writing proficiently
         4) A simple process to learn and execute

C. Future Possibilities of Computer Programs for Writing

   1. Rapid change
   2. Improved programs

3. Increased use and availability
4. More realistic assessment of value—critical work
   (i.e., reading age level)

Chapter Nine

CONQUERING TESTS

This is the point of education. To direct a student's attention toward that which, at first, exceeds his grasp, but whose compelling stature and fascination will draw him after it. Simplification, leveling, watering down as they now prevail in all but the most privileged education is criminal. They condescend fatally to the capacities unbeknown within us. Attacks on so-called elitism mask a vulgar condescension: toward all those judged a priori to be incapable of better things. Both thought and love ask too much of us. They humble us. —— George Steiner

Educators who say "Don't grade them; don't label them. You have to make them feel good about themselves," cause the problems. It makes no sense for students to be full of self-esteem if they have learned nothing. Reality will soon puncture their illusions, and they will have to face two disturbing facts: that they are ignorant, and that the adults responsible for teaching them have lied to them.
—— Paul Vitz

In a growing number of educational contexts, the idea of giving grades and taking tests has fallen out of favor. Many educators and schools are influenced by a progressive educational philosophy and the tenets of the self-esteem movement. When students are given the choice of taking the course "pass/fail," they generally are acknowledging that they are taking the course less seriously. In the end, this sets the student up for failure, because this is not how reality and the real world works. Being tested on what you know and can do is a routine part of adult life.

People will never get away from being tested. Tests and taking tests will follow you throughout your life. It is not just an experience of school; it is a regular pattern of life. So it is best to master the art of taking tests and not freaking out over them.

Tests are a tool to evaluate the student's mastery of the material. Schools should be committed to objective, national measures of academic mastery, such as advanced placement or international baccalaureate standards. Ideally, a student's grades will be benchmarked to these international objective academic standards and not subject to the whims of a given instructor or capability of a given school. There are three major factors that determine a student's grade in a course: 1) homework, 2) tests, and 3) teacher relationship. To get good grades a student must learn to excel in all three areas.

Homework

Homework is a method used to learn 70 percent of the subject material. The other 30 percent is learned in class. If a student doesn't pay attention in class, he or she must depend much more on homework. However, if a student doesn't do homework, the chances of passing tests are greatly lessened because the student has avoided ownership of the learning process.

The purpose of school is learning. The purpose of class is for a student to be exposed to new material and to clarify the student's initial questions and the purpose of homework is to give the student the opportunity to learn the material. In class, the teacher teaches—exposing the student to new concepts and material. At home the student learns, developing facility with these concepts so that they can be used later. *Therefore, homework is ultimately more important than classwork. It is the instructor's responsibility to teach the material. It is the student's responsibility to learn the material.* Homework should ideally raise new questions in the mind of the student as the student takes responsibility to learn the material. If homework is neglected, this feedback loop is broken and the student loses.

Tests

1. Keys to Basic Improvement
   - Practice – do homework under a time deadline
   - Prepare – train as an athlete for a major competition

     "Preparation in practice leads to game day success." — Ara Parseghian, legendary Notre Dame football coach

     "The lesson from championship teams is that they never take a game or an opponent for granted. They realize the importance of each game and prepare the same way, whether the opponent is strong or weak. They have a goal of doing their best at all times and reaping the rewards of winning." — Ron Kurtus

   - Produce – have confidence and learn from mistakes

2. Physiological Preparation
   - No heavy meals
   - Regular exercise
   - Get six to eight hours of sleep
   - Get up two hours before the test
   - Avoid medication, if possible

3. Strategic Preparation (Preparing for the Fight)
   - Study the material by sections.
   - Get the big picture clearly, key definitions, and major relationships particularly between the big ideas.

- Write sample questions (bias handouts, headings, and summaries).
- Study in a group only for practice, not for learning or reviewing.
- Avoid cramming by doing regular review.

4. Tactical Preparation (Engaged in Fight)
   - Anticipate the type of test
     - Essay
     - Short Answer
     - Multiple Choice
     - List
     - Memory
     - Document Based Question (DBQ)
   - Look over the test quickly when it is first handed out so as to better manage your time usage.
   - Anticipate the time needed for each section.
   - Start with the section you know best.
   - Do not change your first response to a multiple choice question.
   - Read the question before reading the comprehension paragraph.
   - Write quick short outlines for all essay questions.
   - Avoid lengthy paragraphs or rephrasing the question; teachers can spot fillers used when the student doesn't know the answer.

5. Essay Tests
   - Analyze the question
     - Describe (adjectives and adverbs)
     - Compare (similarities and differences)
     - Explain (substantiating an opinion)
     - Contrast (comparison of differences)
     - Discuss (open-ended track class discussion)
     - Argue (point of view—evidence matters most)

- Write a thesis based on the question (take a clear position).
- Write an outline.
- Underline key facts used to support your thesis in your answer—this helps the teacher in grading.
- Organize the essay for easy reading and clarity of argument—this too helps the teacher during grading.
- Keep sentences short.
- Neatness counts.
- Conclude with long-term implications that suggest complexity and ambiguity that extend beyond the immediate question.

6. Cheating or Plagiarism—Don't.
   - Faked Illness
   - Honor Code

   "I pledge before God and the school community that this work reflects my own intellectual effort and that no unauthorized help has been given or received."

   - Academic Integrity Committee (Cyber-Plagiarism)
   - Honor Council
   - Transcript

Teacher Relationships

1. Students determine teacher relationships.

2. Teachers are looking for students who are serious about learning, not students who have a high aptitude for the subject.

3. Classroom decorum is the source of a teacher's initial assessment of a student's attitude. A negative reputation

can impact a student's college recommendations years later.

4. Be cordial and respectful of a teacher—even if you do not like him or her. Though sometimes difficult, it is an important lesson for life, as encountering bosses or authority figures you dislike will be the case in almost every business of future life situation.

5. A personal relationship with a teacher can influence a student's grade. It may seem unfair, but it is a fact.

Big Idea
1. The key to test performance is homework performance.
2. The key to test performance is regular review—as opposed to cramming—and practice.
3. *The purpose of a test is to show what has been previously learned, not to learn the material again or for the first time!*

Action Steps
1. Short-Term: Evaluate your past test performances and determine what kind of tests are proving to be the most difficult for you. Develop a plan to address this weakness.

2. Long-Term: Prior to a test, write up a sample test over the material. Make it difficult, but fair.

Playing Up: Setting the Horizon of Expectation

It is one thing to be a big fish in a small pond and quite another thing to be a big fish in a large pond. Setting matters.

I recently visited a new Christian high school whose classroom and athletic facilities are head turning. General appearances were enough to confirm the school's overall commitment to excellence. The football stadium itself was so superior that the local NFL team used it for their informal summer practices during a lockout.

But facilities only told half the story. This school had won two state championships in football in the previous two years and notably had done so while playing up. This was a 3A school playing in a 4A league. The decision to play up was a conscious one by the administration. It meant that their athletes would be faced with better competition, would have to train harder, be better coached, and shun the temptation to play and think small. The horizon of expectation was set. They made every effort to meet it without excuse. And evidently they did so with great success. Playing up has its costs and its rewards.

This is *not* how most Christian schools function.

Most Christian schools' athletic programs are marginally better than a church or homeschool league. The expectations are low, as are the results. In many Christian schools, easier academic assessments are deliberately chosen to make the school look better than it really is. Rather than compare themselves with academically aspiring schools, instead they compare themselves to inner-city public schools that are racked by a multitude of factors that reduce achievement. In the comparison game, one can either compare oneself with the best or the worst. That decision establishes the horizon of expectation for all involved in the institution both academically and athletically.

There are three reasons why Christian schools are prone to compare themselves with weaker institutions and lower metrics of achievement: populism, subjectivism, and compartmentalism.

Many conservative Christians are suspicious of, if not allergic to, any hint of elitism. It's a dirty word, belying their habitual cultural disposition to lowbrow populism. Historian Nathan Hatch writes, "What then is the driving force behind American Christianity if it is not the quality of its organizations, the status of its clergy, or the power of its intellectual life?... [A] central force has been its democratic or populist orientation." There are the obligatory references to "excellence" on the Christian school website and in their marketing material. But there are few systemic commitments to make excellence a lived reality. "No child left behind" has morphed into an excuse to lower standards and inflate grades. In a different time, University of Chicago president Robert Hutchin's argued "The best education for the few is the best education for all." Raising expectations, aspiring to excellence, and encountering ennobling truths—this is the aim of great education. Modern people are too satisfied with mundane existence, with the lowest common denominator of human aspiration. Making ourselves the measure of all, we have lost the heroic imagination. Narcissistic pride has replaced aspirational humility. We have a weakened sense of ideals and idealism. Cambridge University professor George Steiner pleads for the alternative.

This is the point of education. To direct a student's attention toward that which, at first, exceeds his grasp, but whose compelling stature and fascination will draw him after it. Simplification, leveling, watering down as they now prevail in all but the most privileged education is criminal. They condescend fatally to the capacities unbeknown within us. Attacks on so-called elitism mask a vulgar condescension: toward all those judged *a priori* to be incapable of better things. Both thought and love ask too much of us. They humble us.

Students cannot imagine their own potential. They are incapable of establishing the horizons of their own expectations. They cannot imagine the fruit of a life lived out of a cultivated mind, captivated imagination, and ordered loves. It is not only beyond their grasp, it's sadly beyond their imagining. They may aspire to be a contestant on *American Idol*, but few appreciate the discipline needed to cultivate a latent musical talent.

A lottery mindset has contaminated our understanding of mastery. Ours is a superficial and ephemeral culture where celebrities become famous for being famous, a culture where success, like the lottery, is expected to be instant and unearned. In schools where the "pride of not doing well" is pervasive among students, where academic content is derided among teachers, where hard work is distained among parents, and TV establishes the heights of public discourse, the cultural prerequisites of an educated mind are lost.

Christian schools should make no apology; education is intrinsically elitist. *New York Times* journalist William Henry writes, "Schools exist to teach, to test, to rank hierarchically, to promote the idea that knowing and understanding more is better than knowing and understanding less." To deny this fact is to deny reality.

Christian schools celebrate Lewis, Tolkien, and Chesterton, but we somehow give students the impression that their genius and Christian mind was innate rather than cultivated over a lifetime of disciplined study, selective mentorship, and daily habits. In doing so, we teach a lie, and distort their views and practice.

It's time to let people fail, to hold students accountable, to resist grade inflation, to celebrate the hard teacher and the tough principal. We do no one a favor by giving young people the impression that discipline, hard work, and perseverance aren't necessary ingredients for success.

Won't children be left behind? Here's C.S. Lewis' answer:

> "And what," you ask, "about the dull boy? What about our Tommy, who is so highly strung and doesn't like doing sums and grammar? Is he to be brutally sacrificed to other people's sons?" I answer: Dear Madam, you quite misunderstand Tommy's real wishes and real interests. It is the "aristocratic" system, which will really give Tommy what he wants. If you let me have my way, Tommy will gravitate very comfortably to the bottom of the form; and there he will sit at the back of the room chewing caramels and conversing *sotto voce* with his peers, occasionally ragging and occasionally getting punished, and all the time imbibing that playful intransigent attitude to authority which is our chief protection against England becoming a servile State. When he grows up he will not be a genius, but the world will still have room for a great many more Tommies than geniuses. There are dozens of jobs (much better paid than intellectual ones) in which he can be very useful and happy. And one priceless benefit he will enjoy: he will know he's not clever. The distinction between him and the great brains will have been clear to him ever since, in

the playground, he punched the heads containing those great brains. He will have a certain, half amused respect for them. He will cheerfully admit that, though he could knock spots off them on the golf links, they know and do what he cannot.

We need to put the brutal honesty of *American Idol* judge Simon Cowell in the classroom and once again call a spade a spade. If we don't now, later reality will. Playing down will not get us there.

And then there is the matter of subjectivism, the relativism of standards coupled with the assumptions of self-esteem. American schools have built an industry on promoting self-esteem as a means of increasing academic achievement with the sad result that American students now "feel" good about being dumb, when the only consistent correlation of academic achievement is student effort. New York University psychologist Paul Vitz writes,

> Educators who say "Don't grade them, don't label them, you have to make them feel good about themselves," cause these problems. It makes no sense for students to be full of self-esteem if they have learned nothing. Reality will soon puncture their illusions and they will have to face two disturbing facts: that they are ignorant, and that the adults responsible for teaching them have lied to them.

There are no short cuts to learning. When researchers Brophy and Good examined teacher behavior and student achievement over five years, they found that it was content, core-knowledge, teacher-driven instruction, and drill and practice methods, that made the difference—namely, traditional educational approaches.[6]

---

[6] E.D. Hirsch, Jr. *The Schools We Need: And Why We Don't Have Them* (Anchor, 1999).

As long as students are made the measure of their own learning, as is typically the case in progressive pedagogy, as long as research-based objective standards are frowned upon, as long as the weakest assessment tools are preferred over those that assume high standards, students will rise to meet the low expectations to their own demise. Christian education is meant for more. Certainly, Christ and his kingdom deserve more.

During my tumultuous tenure as headmaster of the Cambridge School of Dallas, I advocated for single-track education. Mastery was our goal for every student. Every course and the entire scope and sequence was benchmarked to the terminus Advanced Placement standard in the discipline. The choice of the AP curriculum was arbitrary, but the commitment to external curricular standards to which every teacher and student could be held accountable was not.

Skeptics of this approach should consider the 1988 film, *Stand and Deliver*, that illustrates the real-life story of Jaime Escalante who challenged his Latino students in an East Los Angeles high school to take the AP Calculus exam. In 1982, eigtheen students at Garfield High School took and passed the exam. By 1987, through the encouragement of their teachers, 155 students were taking the exam each year. Somebody needs to be the first person to step up and raise expectations.

To paraphrase C.S. Lewis in his essay, "The Poison of Subjectivism," unless there is some objective standard of curricular mastery that overarches the whims of students, parents, administrators, and boards alike—whether any of us follow them or not—then anything goes in the classroom. The game is over. We are ceding the fact that Christian education has no distinctive advantage in education. Mastery becomes subjective—or more accurately, mastery becomes that which is decided by any particular educational expert who happens to be in power. Lewis was correct when he said, "Unless the measuring rod is independent of the things measured, we can do no measuring."

There is a widespread educational complaint against the over emphasis on teaching to the test, to accountability, and outcome-based merit pay and the like. There is a point to some of these concerns—a bureaucratic overreaction to an educational culture that despises accountability and objective standards. At some point American education will wake up when it realizes that it is not OK to be ranked well below other industrialized nations in literacy and numeracy. Scores from the 2009 Program for International Student Assessment show fifteen-year-old students in the US performing about average in reading and science, and below average in math. Out of thirty-four countries, the U.S. ranked fourteenth in reading, seventeenth in science and twenty-fifth in math (*USA Today,* December 7, 2010). Thomas Friedman warns, "Do you homework or you will soon be working for the Chinese." China, Korea, and India are countries where educational achievement is still culturally valued. There are many places in the world where hierarchy and objective standards still count and where student aspirations are calibrated accordingly. There are many countries in the world where playing up remains an honored tradition. The widespread negative reaction to Yale law professor Amy Chua's book *Battle Hymn of the Tiger Mother,* is an example of what is at stake in the wider educational world. The "Lake Wobegon effect" is a national phenomenon—"where everyone is assumed to be above average and all the children are good looking." Morris Berman warns, "In an upside-down world, *all* quality is going to be viewed as elitist." This is a perversion of what education demands. C.S. Lewis wisely reminds us that

> Equality has no place in the life of the mind. Beauty is not democratic; she reveals herself more to the few than to the many, more to the persistent and disciplined

seekers than to the careless. Virtue is not democratic; she is achieved by those who pursue her more hotly than most men. Truth is not democratic; she demands special talents and special industry in those to whom she gives her favors. Political democracy is doomed if it tries to extend its demands for equality into these higher spheres. Ethical, intellectual, or aesthetic democracy is death.

Golf is not golf without par. We play down when we lower standards or abandon them all together. Ours is an age that willfully does both. Novelist and literary critic Cynthia Ozick observes, "Distinction-making, even distinction-discerning, is largely in decline. The difference between high and low is valued by few and blurred by most." Christian schools must be places that create a counter-cultural ethos, because of our commitment to objective truth as an accurate assessment of reality and human nature. Lewis observes, "There is in all men a tendency to resent the existence of what is stronger, subtler, or better than themselves. In uncorrected and brutal men this hardens into an implacable and disinterested hatred for every kind of excellence." This tendency is not OK in Christian schools.

Finally, there is the tendency to compartmentalize our world to our own religious ghetto. No longer confident that Christianity is the truth about reality, we compartmentalize religion to the margins of life making it a harmless hobby that in the words of Theodore Roszak is "privately engaging, but socially irrelevant." We make low-budget movies for faith-based audiences that win awards that we give to ourselves, because we don't have the confidence, will, or resources to make a difference at the Sundance Film Festival or Hollywood Oscars. Talking only to ourselves we have abdicated our responsibility to make a cultural difference. The dictates of pluralism require a greater recognition of how, where, and who shapes culture. Cocooning into our own religious lifestyle enclaves with our own forms of entertainment and awards will further the irrelevance of the biblical vision of life in society. If the church league is our standard, we will never make the major league. The Amish are quaint, but not influential. Christians run the risk of being quaint and culturally irrelevant.

Some might take a call for wider cultural engagement as an excuse to abandon distinctively Christian schooling. Nothing could be further from the case. I am not questioning the substance of what we teach, but the scope of our influence. One would assume that those who teach an accurate understanding of reality with a pedagogy based on an accurate assessment of human nature would have better results in practice than those who teach some variant of a false worldview and inadequate anthropology. It is time to regain our confidence in what we teach. Philosopher Dallas Willard writes that Christian education institutions "do not present the basic points of the Christian faith as constituting a body of Christian knowledge that Christians have and non-Christian institutions do not have." He goes on:

> Until institutions of Christian higher education [the same is true for K-12 education] and their faculties break out of the posture that holds genuine knowledge to be secular, and until they carry out their task of developing and conveying distinctively Christian knowledge—in the free, open, and rational manner that characterizes the life of the mind and scholarship at its ideal best—those institutions will, despite all appearances, be a primary *hindrance* to the "Jesus project" on earth.

We need to be leading in the education debates, not following. The US Secretary of Education should be calling Christian school associations to ask them how they are achieving so much with so little. Instead, we talk to ourselves, marginalize our relevance, and exhibit insecurity in our "religious" convictions as if they are not foundational to what is real and what works. We have played the victim for too long. Willard writes that the focus of discipleship is not the church, but the world. It is on that stage alone where the quality of our mettle is to be tested. We were made for more than the Christian ghetto.

The future challenge of Christian schooling is to have such confidence in our mission based as it is on an accurate assessment of reality and human nature that we are willing to rise to the highest international standards, to be held accountable to best practices, and in general to play up to the national educational debate. We must expand the horizons of expectations for our administrators, teachers, parents, and students. We know what it means to play up in football. It's time, if not past time, to play up as schools.

This article was first published in Building a Better School: Essays on Exemplary Christian School Leadership, *edited by Timothy P. Wiens and Kathryn L. Wiens (Paideia Press, 2012) and is used here with permission.*

Chapter Ten

THE BODY OF A STUDENT

Keep your vitality. A life without health is like a river without water. — Maxime Lagacé

Doctors won't make you healthy. Nutritionists won't make you slim. Teachers won't make you smart. Gurus won't make you calm. Mentors won't make you rich. Trainers won't make you fit. Ultimately, you have to take responsibility. Save yourself. — Naval Ravikant

Too few schools take into consideration the lived context of the student, which inevitably impacts his or her ability to learn. Is there enough food at home? Is there marital discord at home? Is the student having relationship problems? Is the student getting enough sleep? All of these factors impact whether a student can learn. The school has a responsibility to pay attention to these extracurricular factors in their students.

1. *Pay attention to your body.* A student's performance, like that of an athlete, is only as good as he or she is physically prepared. Hunger, fatigue, illness, and emotional trauma will influence a student's ability to learn in class and perform on a test. Serious academic as well as athletic competitors pay close attention to every aspect of their performance—but especially to their bodies.

2. *Get involved with a sport or exercise.* Athletic participation almost always improves a student's grades.

3. *Use good health practices.* Missing school due to illness will only make your efforts more difficult. Avoid it whenever possible. Get a flu shot each year.

4. *Fuel up.* Eat breakfast—particularly protein (a protein shake is a quick easy meal).

5. *Watch fatigue.* Particularly watch out for staying up too late on Saturday night, as the impact of staying up will catch up with you after the first day, that is, on Monday morning. Fatigue makes everything harder and is a major cause of discouragement and depression. Rest is a critical aspect of doing well in school.

6. *Practice the Sabbath.* Use a Sabbath rest by preparing for Monday on Saturday.

7. *Take vitamins.* Especially Vitamin C and Zinc.

8. *Don't do all-nighters.* Avoid staying up all night to study for a test. (Note: we have all done it!)

9. *Keep your target in sight.* Set clear academic goals each term and place them in a prominent location in your room for daily review. Discuss these goals with your parents and enlist their help in accountability.

10. *Embrace short-term opportunities in the light of long-term goals.* Get a college pennant of your favorite college or university and place it in your room.

Big Ideas
1. Your ability to learn is only as good as your health and your calmness of mind. Neither are a given.

2. Pay attention to the other lifestyle habits that impact your ability to learn and succeed in school.
3. When possible, avoid emotional drama.

Action Steps
1. Short-Term: Go to bed earlier on Saturday night. Saturday-night activities show up as Monday-morning fatigue.

2. Long-Term: Develop better eating habits (don't skip breakfast), get thirty minutes of exercise every day, and no fewer than six hours of sleep each night.

Chapter Eleven

DOUBLE STUDY

Our commitment to Jesus can stand on no other foundation than a recognition that he is the one who knows the truth about our lives and our universe. It is not possible to trust Jesus, or anyone else, in matter where we do not believe him to be competent.... "Jesus is Lord" can mean little in practice for anyone who has to hesitate before saying, "Jesus is smart."
— Dallas Willard

Anyone who can find a better way than Jesus, he would be the first to tell you to take it. — Dallas Willard

At some point every person has to make their life-defining beliefs their own. They can no longer naively ride on the coattails of their parents' beliefs. They can no longer assume the correctness of their upbringing. Personal ownership of your defining beliefs and worldview is a mark of maturity.

This can be a scary prospect. But intellectual and spiritual integrity both demand it. If Christianity is true, it is true because it reflects reality. It is an honest affirmation of what is. We should desire to align ourselves with an honest assessment of human nature and reality.

Many Christian schools do not encourage this process of spiritual intellectual ownership. They simply appeal to authority—their own authority or that of the Scriptures—and provide no basis for questioning or doubt. This is unfortunate. Living in a pluralistic society, even if you attend a Christian school and lives in a

Christian bubble, an alleged spiritual safety zone, you will be challenged by alternative beliefs and by persons whom you respect who disagree with some of your most precious beliefs. All believers must be open to having their beliefs challenged and questioned. All believers should take their own doubts and questions seriously. Doubt is to be encouraged, not denied. It is a call for deeper study and more reflection.

All truth is God's truth regardless of its source. This means that all knowledge needs to be evaluated as to its truthfulness— whether it is from a non-Christian or Christian source. This is true for knowledge received at a Christian school as much as knowledge received from a public high school or secular college. We need not take it on the word of another or assume something to be truth because it is delivered by an officially sanctioned authority. Being a Christian student demands discernment: being able to decipher the worldview of an argument, its internal logical coherence, and its correspondence to live reality.

This puts the Christian student in a position to need to do "double study." You must first determine what is being said, and second you must determine the truthfulness of the statement and its relationship to a biblical perspective. What is being said and how does this align to Jesus's view on this topic? Theologian J. Gresham Machen wrote,

> The Christian cannot be satisfied so long as any human activity is either opposed to Christianity or out of all connection with Christianity. Christianity must pervade not merely all nations, but also all of human thought. The Christian, therefore, cannot be indifferent to any branch of earnest human endeavor. It must all be brought into some relation to the gospel. It must be studied either in order to be demonstrated as false, or else in order to be made useful in advancing the Kingdom of

God. The Kingdom must be advanced not merely extensively, but also intensively. The Church must seek to conquer not merely every man for Christ, but also the whole of man.

There are only three basic approaches to reality. Bruno Munari was one of the greatest graphic designers of the twentieth century. He argued that the basic building block of design is based on three shapes: squares, circles, and triangles. It is also true that every book and all of human thought can be reduced to one of three basic approaches to reality: naturalistic, pantheistic, or theistic. As a Christian student, you must learn to determine the perspective being used by the teacher or the textbook.

The naturalistic perspective suggests that reality is to be found outside of yourself, but is limited by what you can see, measure, and repeat according to the general methods and limits of the scientific method. This perspective is symbolized by a square, a "world without windows."

The pantheistic perspective suggests that the deepest aspect of reality is found in your own divine spark. Reality is found by looking within. This is an increasingly popular approach, especially within popular culture, such as in *Star Wars*. Here reality is not a secular world without windows but is composed at its deepest level by a divine spiritual force. This perspective is symbolized by a circle.

The theistic perspective is a combination of the previous two perspectives. Reality is more than material: there is the divine like pantheism, but it is a reality outside of oneself like naturalism. You can connect to this spiritual reality, but it is from a source outside of yourself. Here the spiritual enters into our reality from the outside. This is the principle of incarnation. Distinctive from both naturalism and pantheism, this spiritual source is personal and therefore involves a relationship. More than making an impersonal connection, like plugging into an electric socket, this kind of connection involves love. This perspective is symbolized by a triangle or the Trinity.

There is obviously a lot more that can be said about these three approaches toward reality. But what is true is that there are only these three. Christian students must be able to assess what they are reading and study critically to determine what basic assumptions about the nature of reality are being made. This always involves "double study." It is not enough to simply learn what is being presented. You must go beyond that to ascertain its point of view and truthfulness. This means that a Christian student must do more than simply learn what is being taught. They must also approach the material being taught, whether by Christians or non-Christians, with discernment. In the end, this will make them far better students.

I learned the necessity of this in college. I attended a small liberal arts college that had a required core course for all students. When I attended, it was called the Heritage of Western Man sequence. It is now called IDEAS: Individual Development: Encounter with the Arts and Sciences. It was an excellent course, but intellectually challenging for Christian students with naive beliefs. Because every student had to take this course, it uniquely shaped the culture of the campus. Freshman students were immediately confronted with Bultmann's critical theory, Freud's psychology, Kuhn's view of paradigms, Sartre's existentialism, as well as the Greeks and Romans. Few students had the tools to intellectually and spiritually handle this material. Consequently, many students' Christian beliefs were challenged and later abandoned after a semester or two of this instruction coupled with the inherent social freedom of college life and inherent adolescent rebellion. A number of Christian students decided to address the challenge to faith in what was being presented by the secular faculty. We worked with seminary professors and Christian authors and professors to develop a supplemental reading list designed specifically for these three courses paralleling the syllabuses.

For each reading, we developed an alternative reading list to help Christian students navigate what they were learning. This supplemental curriculum was placed on reserve in the library. Study groups were developed with the promise that attendance would help students get an A in this mandatory course. It was our experience that without conscious "double study," students would systematically lose their faith. One's studies are not necessarily a safe place. They are an intellectual and spiritual battlefield for the orientation of your mind and the loyalty of your life. This step is not to be taken lightly. J. Gresham Machen was correct when he wrote, "The Christian cannot be satisfied so long as any human activity is either opposed to Christianity or out of all connection with Christianity. Christianity must pervade not merely all nations, but also all of human thought. The Christian, therefore, cannot be indifferent to any branch of earnest human endeavor. It must all be brought into some relation to the gospel." This is double study.

Big Idea
1. A Christian student needs to make his or her beliefs their own.
2. A Christian student needs to take doubt and questions seriously.
3. A Christian student needs to study with discernment.
4. A Christian student needs to do double study.

Action Steps

1. Short-Term: Write a list of your core questions about your beliefs.

2. Long-Term: Explore these questions with an older mentor.

Mixed Signals, Mixed Results

Schools and Christian attitudes toward education reflect a general crisis in the evangelical church—an unwillingness to take apprenticeship to Jesus seriously and a kingdom purpose as the defining characteristic of life.

1. Failure to obey the Great Commission—converts vs. disciples
2. Failure to understand the requirements of apprenticeship to Jesus
3. Failure to understand that our loves govern behavior
4. Failure to see apprenticeship as touching every aspect of life
5. Failure to promote a passion to become like Jesus
6. Failure to understand and resist the patterns of culture
7. Failure to prepare for engagement outside the evangelical ghetto
8. Failure to demonstrate a conversational relationship with Jesus
9. Failure to put service to God's kingdom as a priority
10. Failure to understand the components of a Christian mind

Consequently, we have schools that instruct but don't transform. We get out of our schools exactly what they are designed to produce: a pop-culture version of Christianity Lite coupled with the American Dream of personal peace and affluence.

Most Christians have their children in government schools because they don't see education as being intrinsic to discipleship and beliefs intrinsic to behavior.

Most Christian schools offer a Christianized version of government schools.

Look at the graduates of our schools: Are Christian-school graduates serious about becoming like Jesus and serving him and his kingdom?

Christian schools typically promote social conformity in service of a prolonged altar call in a safe place. The results from such a school is hypocrisy and legalism in service of superficial conversion that is limited to the spheres of parental and administrative control—in effect, an education that does not touch the heart and loves of the student. In contrast, prophetic Christian schools create strategically prepared cultural change agents.

Marks of a Prophetic School
1. Graduates with a Christian perspective on reality
2. Graduates who have learned to live from the resources of heaven
3. Graduates who have skills in analysis both in the social and natural world
4. Graduates who have skills in poetic knowledge in service of empathy
5. Graduates who have a clear understanding of calling
6. Graduates who have a global perspective

As the cultural challenge to faith rises, this is the unique opportunity and calling of Christian schooling.

Christianity and Culture

J. Gresham Machen

In the summer of 1971, when I was at the age of eighteen, my father took me to L'Abri in Switzerland. As a family we were returning from the mission field in Korea on furlough and returned via Europe. During a brief meeting with Dr. Francis Schaeffer, I was handed a small booklet containing this short address, "Christianity and Culture." More than anything else I have read other than the Bible, these words set the course of my life. Here was a call to arms—a call to bring the gospel to bear on every aspect of life and culture. Machen wrote,

> *The Christian cannot be satisfied so long as any human activity is either opposed to Christianity or out of all connection with Christianity. Christianity must pervade not merely all nations, but also all of human thought. The Christian, therefore, cannot be indifferent to any branch of earnest human endeavor. It must all be brought into some relation to the gospel. It must be studied either in order to be demonstrated as false, or else in order to be made useful in advancing the Kingdom of God. The Kingdom must be advanced not merely extensively, but also intensively. The Church must seek to conquer not merely every man for Christ, but also the whole of man.*

For the first time, schooling made sense. I was preparing for battle, a battle for the hearts and minds of individuals and culture. The original address was delivered at Princeton Theological Seminary on September 20, 1912.

Two Tendencies

One of the greatest of the problems that have agitated the Church is the problem of the relation between knowledge and piety, between culture and Christianity. This problem has appeared first of all in the presence of two tendencies in the Church—the scientific or *academic tendency*, and what may be called the *practical tendency*. Some men have devoted themselves chiefly to the task of forming right conceptions as to Christianity and its foundations. To them no fact, however trivial, has appeared worthy of neglect; by them truth has been cherished for its own sake, without immediate reference to practical consequences. Some, on the other hand, have emphasized the essential simplicity of the gospel. The world is lying in misery, we ourselves are sinners, and men are perishing in sin every day. The gospel is the sole means of escape; let us preach it to the world while yet we may. So desperate is the need that we have no time to engage in vain babblings or old wives' fables. While we are discussing the exact location of the churches of Galatia, men are perishing under the curse of the law; while we are settling the date of Jesus' birth, the world is doing without its Christmas message.

The representatives of both of these tendencies regard themselves as Christians, but too often there is little brotherly feeling between them. The Christian of academic tastes accuses his brother of undue emotionalism, of shallow argumentation, of cheap methods of work. On the other hand, your practical man is ever loud in his denunciation of academic indifference to the dire needs of humanity. The scholar is represented either as a dangerous disseminator of doubt, or else as a man whose faith is a faith without works. A man who investigates human sin and the grace of God by the aid solely of dusty volumes, carefully secluded in a warm and comfortable study, without a thought of the men who are perishing in misery every day!

But if the problem appears thus in the presence of different tendencies in the Church, it becomes yet far more insistent within the consciousness of the individual. If we are thoughtful, we must see that the desire to know and the desire to be saved are widely different. The scholar must apparently assume the attitude of an impartial observer—an attitude which seems absolutely impossible to the pious Christian laying hold upon Jesus as the only Savior from the load of sin. If these two activities—on the one hand the acquisition of knowledge, and on the other the exercise and inculcation of simple faith—are both to be given a place in our lives, the question of their proper relationship cannot be ignored.

Segregating Thinking from Faith

The problem is made for us the more difficult of solution because we are unprepared for it. Our whole system of school and college education is so constituted as to keep religion and culture as far apart as possible and ignore the question of the relationship between them. On five or six days in the week, we were engaged in the acquisition of knowledge. From this activity the study of religion was banished. We studied natural science without considering its bearing or lack of bearing upon natural theology or upon revelation. We studied Greek without opening the New Testament. We studied history with careful avoidance of that greatest of historical movements which was ushered in by the preaching of Jesus. In philosophy, the vital importance of the study for religion could not entirely be concealed, but it was kept as far as possible in the background. On Sundays, on the other hand, we had religious instruction that called for little exercise of the intellect.

Careful preparation for Sunday-school lessons as for lessons in mathematics or Latin was unknown. Religion seemed to be something that had to do only with the emotions and the will, leaving the intellect to secular studies. What wonder that after such training we came to regard religion and culture as belonging to two entirely separate compartments of the soul, and their union as involving the destruction of both?

Upon entering the Seminary, we are suddenly introduced to an entirely different procedure. Religion is suddenly removed from its seclusion; the same methods of study are applied to it as were formerly reserved for natural science and for history. We study the Bible no longer solely with the desire of moral and spiritual improvement, but also in order to know. Perhaps the first impression is one of infinite loss. The scientific spirit seems to be replacing simple faith, the mere apprehension of dead facts to be replacing the practice of principles. The difficulty is perhaps not so much that we are brought face to face with new doubts as to the truth of Christianity. Rather is it the conflict of method, of spirit that troubles us. The scientific spirit seems to be incompatible with the old spirit of simple faith. *In short, almost entirely unprepared, we are brought face to face with the problem of the relationship between knowledge and piety, or, otherwise expressed, between culture and Christianity.*

Option One: Culture Over Christianity
This problem may be settled in one of three ways. *In the first place, Christianity may be subordinated to culture.* That solution really, though to some extent unconsciously, is being favored by a very large and influential portion of the Church today. For the elimination of the supernatural in Christianity—so tremendously common today—really makes Christianity merely natural. Christianity becomes a human product, a mere part of human culture. But as such it is something entirely different from the old Christianity that was based upon a direct revelation from God. Deprived thus of its note of authority, the gospel is no gospel any longer; it is a check for untold millions—but without the signature at the bottom. So in subordinating Christianity to culture we have

really destroyed Christianity, and what continues to bear the old name is a counterfeit.

Option Two: Christianity Over Culture

The second solution goes to the opposite extreme. In its effort to give religion a clear field, it seeks to destroy culture. This solution is better than the first. Instead of indulging in a shallow optimism or deification of humanity, it recognizes the profound evil of the world, and does not shrink from the most heroic remedy. The world is so evil that it cannot possibly produce the means for its own salvation. Salvation must be the gift of an entirely new life, coming directly from God. Therefore, it is argued, the culture of this world must be a matter at least of indifference to the Christian. Now in its extreme form this solution hardly requires refutation. If Christianity is really found to contradict that reason which is our only means of apprehending truth, then of course we must either modify or abandon Christianity. We cannot therefore be entirely independent of the achievements of the intellect. Furthermore, we cannot without inconsistency employ the printing-press, the railroad, the telegraph in the propagation of our gospel, and at the same time denounce as evil those activities of the human mind that produced these things. And in the production of these things not merely practical inventive genius had a part, but also, back of that, the investigations of pure science animated simply by the desire to know. In its extreme form, therefore, involving the abandonment of all intellectual activity, this second solution would be adopted by none of us. But very many pious men in the Church today are adopting this solution in essence and in spirit. They admit that the Christian must have a part in human culture. But they regard such activity as a necessary evil—a dangerous and unworthy task necessary to be gone through with under a stern sense of duty in order that thereby the higher ends of the gospel may be attained. Such men can never engage in the arts and sciences with anything like enthusiasm—such enthusiasm they would regard as disloyalty to the gospel. Such a

153

position is really both illogical and unbiblical. God has given us certain powers of mind, and has implanted within us the ineradicable conviction that these powers were intended to be exercised. The Bible, too, contains poetry that exhibits no lack of enthusiasm, no lack of a keen appreciation of beauty. With this second solution of the problem we cannot rest content. Despite all we can do, the desire to know and the love of beauty cannot be entirely stifled, and we cannot permanently regard these desires as evil.

Option Three: Consecration of Culture

Are then Christianity and culture in a conflict that is to be settled only by the destruction of one or the other of the contending forces? *A third solution, fortunately, is possible—namely consecration.* Instead of destroying the arts and sciences or being indifferent to them, let us cultivate them with all the enthusiasm of the veriest humanist, but at the same time consecrate them to the service of our God. Instead of stifling the pleasures afforded by the acquisition of knowledge or by the appreciation of what is beautiful, let us accept these pleasures as the gifts of a heavenly Father. *Instead of obliterating the distinction between the Kingdom and the world, or on the other hand withdrawing from the world into a sort of modernized intellectual monasticism, let us go forth joyfully, enthusiastically to make the world subject to God.*

Certain obvious advantages are connected with such a solution of the problem. In the first place, a logical advantage. A man can believe only what he holds to be true. We are Christians because we hold Christianity to be true. But other men hold Christianity to be false. Who is right? That question can be settled only by an examination and comparison of the reasons adduced on both sides. It is true, one of the grounds for our belief is an inward experience that we cannot share—the great experience begun by conviction of sin and conversion and continued by communion with God—an experience, which other men do not possess, and upon, which, therefore, we cannot directly base an argument. But if our position is correct, we ought at least to be able to show the other man that his reasons may be inconclusive. And that involves careful study of both sides of the question. Furthermore, the field of Christianity is the world. *The Christian cannot be satisfied so long as any human activity is either opposed to Christianity or out of all connection with Christianity. Christianity must pervade not merely all nations, but also all of human thought. The Christian, therefore, cannot be indifferent to any branch of earnest human endeavor. It must all be brought into some relation to the gospel. It must be studied either in order to be demonstrated as false, or else in order to be made useful in advancing the Kingdom of God. The Kingdom must be advanced not merely extensively, but also intensively. The Church must seek to conquer not merely every man for Christ, but also the whole of man.* We are accustomed to encourage ourselves in our discouragements by the thought of the time when every knee shall bow and every tongue confess that Jesus is Lord. No less inspiring is the other aspect of that same great consummation. That will also be a time when doubts have disappeared, when every contradiction has been removed, when all of science converges to one great conviction, when all of art is devoted to one great end, when all of human thinking is permeated by the refining, ennobling influence of Jesus, when every thought has been brought into subjection to the obedience of Christ.

Preparing Ground for the Gospel

If to some of our practical men, these advantages of our solution of the problem seem to be intangible, we can point to the merely numerical advantage of intellectual and artistic activity within the Church. We are all agreed that at least one great function of the Church is the conversion of individual men. The missionary movement is the great religious movement of our day. Now it is perfectly true that men must be brought to Christ one by one. There are no laborsaving devices in evangelism. It is all handwork.

155

And yet it would be a great mistake to suppose that all men are equally well prepared to receive the gospel. It is true that the decisive thing is the regenerative power of God. That can overcome all lack of preparation, and the absence of that makes even the best preparation useless. *But as a matter of fact God usually exerts that power in connection with certain prior conditions of the human mind, and it should be ours to create, so far as we can, with the help of God, those favorable conditions for the reception of the gospel. False ideas are the greatest obstacles to the reception of the gospel. We may preach with all the fervor of a reformer and yet succeed only in winning a straggler here and there, if we permit the whole collective thought of the nation or of the world to be controlled by ideas, which, by the resistless force of logic, prevent Christianity from being regarded as anything more than a harmless delusion. Under such circumstances, what God desires us to do is to destroy the obstacle at its root.* Many would have the seminaries combat error by attacking it as it is taught by its popular exponents. Instead of that they confuse their students with a lot of German names unknown outside the walls of the universities. That method of procedure is based simply upon a profound belief in the pervasiveness of ideas. *What is today matter of academic speculation begins tomorrow to move armies and pull down empires. In that second stage, it has gone too far to be combated, the time to stop it was when it was still a matter of impassionate debate. So as Christians we should try to mold the thought of the world in such a way as to make the acceptance of Christianity something more than a logical absurdity.* Thoughtful men are wondering why the students of our great Eastern universities no longer enter the ministry or display any very vital interest in Christianity. Various totally inadequate explanations are proposed, such as the increasing attractiveness of other professions—an absurd explanation, by the way, since other professions are becoming so over-crowded that a man can barely make a living in them. The real difficulty amounts to this—that the thought of the day, as it makes itself most strongly felt in the universities, but from them spreads inevitably to the masses of the people, is profoundly opposed to Christianity, or at least—what is nearly as bad—it is out of all connection with Christianity. The Church is unable either to combat it or to assimilate it, because the Church simply does not understand it. Under such circumstances, what more pressing duty than for those who have received the mighty experience of regeneration, who, therefore, do not, like the world, neglect that whole series of vitally relevant facts which is embraced in Christian experience—what more pressing duty than for these men to make themselves masters of the thought of the world in order to make it an instrument of truth instead of error? The Church has no right to be so absorbed in helping the individual that she forgets the world.

Two Objections

There are two objections to our solution of the problem. If you bring culture and Christianity thus into close union—in the first place, *will not Christianity destroy culture?* Must not art and science be independent in order to flourish? We answer that it all depends upon the nature of their dependence. Subjection to any external authority or even to any human authority would be fatal to art and science. But subjection to God is entirely different. Dedication of human powers to God is found, as a matter of fact, not to destroy but to heighten them. God gave those powers. He understands them well enough not bunglingly to destroy His own gifts. In the second place, *will not culture destroy Christianity?* Is it not far easier to be an earnest Christian if you confine your attention to the Bible and do not risk being led astray by the thought of the world? We answer of course it is easier. Shut yourself up in an intellectual monastery, do not disturb yourself with the thoughts of unregenerate men, and of course you will find it easier to be a Christian, just as it is easier to be a good soldier in comfortable winter quarters than it is on the field of battle. You save your own soul—but the Lord's enemies remain in possession of the field.

But by whom is this task of transforming the unwieldy, resisting mass of human thought until it becomes subservient to the gospel—by whom is this task to be accomplished? To some extent, no doubt, by professors in theological seminaries and universities. But the ordinary minister of the gospel cannot shirk his responsibility. It is a great mistake to suppose that investigation can successfully be carried on by a few specialists whose work is of interest to nobody but themselves. Many men of many minds are needed. What we need first of all, especially in our American churches, is a more general interest in the problems of theological science. Without that, the specialist is without the stimulating atmosphere, which nerves him to do his work.

But no matter what his station in life, the scholar must be a regenerated man—he must yield to no one in the intensity and depth of his religious experience. We are well supplied in the world with excellent scholars who are without that qualification. They are doing useful work in detail, in Biblical philology, in exegesis, in Biblical theology, and in other branches of study. But they are not accomplishing the great task; they are not assimilating modern thought to Christianity, because they are without that experience of God's power in the soul, which is of the essence of Christianity. They have only one side for the comparison. Modern thought they know, but Christianity is really foreign to them. It is just that great inward experience which it is the function of the true Christian scholar to bring into some sort of connection with the thought of the world.

Loss of Cultural Influence
During the last thirty years there has been a tremendous defection from the Christian Church. It is evidenced even by things that lie on the surface. For example, by the decline in church attendance and in Sabbath observance and in the number of candidates for the ministry. Special explanations, it is true, are sometimes given for these discouraging tendencies. But why should we deceive ourselves, why comfort ourselves by palliative explanations? Let us face the facts. *The falling off in church attendance, the neglect of*

Sabbath observance—these things are simply surface indications of a decline in the power of Christianity. Christianity is exerting a far less powerful direct influence in the civilized world today than it was exerting thirty years ago.

What is the cause of this tremendous defection? For my part, I have little hesitation in saying that it lies chiefly in the intellectual sphere. *Men do not accept Christianity because they can no longer be convinced that Christianity is true.* It may be useful, but is it true? Other explanations, of course, are given. The modern defection from the Church is explained by the practical materialism of the age. Men are so much engrossed in making money that they have no time for spiritual things. That explanation has a certain range of validity. But its range is limited. It applies perhaps to the boomtowns of the West, where men are intoxicated by sudden possibilities of boundless wealth. But the defection from Christianity is far broader than that. It is felt in the settled countries of Europe even more strongly than in America. It is felt among the poor just as strongly as among the rich. Finally it is felt most strongly of all in the universities, and that is only one indication more that the true cause of the defection is intellectual. To a very large extent, the students of our great Eastern universities—and still more the universities of Europe—are not Christians. And they are not Christians often just because they are students. The thought of the day, as it makes itself most strongly felt in the universities, is profoundly opposed to Christianity, or at least it is out of connection with Christianity. The chief obstacle to the Christian religion today lies in the sphere of the intellect.

Two Misconceptions
That assertion must be guarded against two misconceptions.

In the first place, I do not mean that most men reject Christianity consciously on account of intellectual difficulties. On the contrary, rejection of Christianity is due in the vast majority of cases simply to indifference. Only a few men have given the subject real attention. The vast majority of those who reject the gospel do so simply because they know nothing about it. But whence comes this indifference? It is due to the intellectual atmosphere in which men are living. The modern world is dominated by ideas, which ignore the gospel. Modern culture is not altogether opposed to the gospel. But it is out of all connection with it. It not only prevents the acceptance of Christianity. It prevents Christianity even from getting a hearing.

In the second place, I do not mean that the removal of intellectual objections will make a man a Christian. No conversion was ever wrought simply by argument. A change of heart is also necessary. And that can be wrought only by the immediate exercise of the power of God. But because intellectual labor is insufficient it does not follow as is so often assumed, that it is unnecessary. God may, it is true, overcome all intellectual obstacles by an immediate exercise of His regenerative power. Sometimes He does. But He does so very seldom. Usually He exerts His power in connection with certain conditions of the human mind. *Usually He does not bring into the Kingdom, entirely without preparation, those whose mind and fancy are completely dominated by ideas, which make the acceptance of the gospel logically impossible.*

Forces of Modern Culture
Modern culture is a tremendous force. It affects all classes of society. It affects the ignorant as well as the learned. What is to be done about it? In the first place the Church may simply withdraw from the conflict. She may simply allow the mighty stream of modern thought to flow by unheeded and do her work merely in the back-eddies of the current. There are still some men in the world who have been unaffected by modern culture. They may still be won for Christ without intellectual labor. And they must be won. It is useful; it is necessary work. If the Church is satisfied with that alone, let her give up the scientific education of her

ministry. Let her assume the truth of her message and learn simply how it may be applied in detail to modern industrial and social conditions. Let her give up the laborious study of Greek and Hebrew. Let her abandon the scientific study of history to the men of the world. In a day of increased scientific interest, let the Church go on becoming less scientific. In a day of increased specialization, of renewed interest in philology and in history, of more rigorous scientific method, let the Church go on abandoning her Bible to her enemies. They will study it scientifically, rest assured, if the Church does not. Let her substitute sociology altogether for Hebrew, practical expertness for the proof of her gospel. Let her shorten the preparation of her ministry; let her permit it to be interrupted, yet more and more, by premature practical activity. By doing so she will win a straggler here and there. But her winnings will be but temporary. The great current of modern culture will sooner or later engulf her puny eddy. God will save her somehow—out of the depths. But the labor of centuries will have been swept away. God grant that the Church may not resign herself to that. God grant she may face her problem squarely and bravely. That problem is not easy. It involves the very basis of her faith. Christianity is the proclamation of an historical fact—that Jesus Christ rose from the dead. Modern thought has no place for that proclamation. It prevents men even from listening to the message. Yet the culture of today cannot simply be rejected as a whole. It is not like the pagan culture of the first century. It is not wholly non-Christian. Much of it has been derived directly from the Bible. There are significant movements in it, going to waste, which might well be used for the defense of the gospel. The situation is complex. Easy wholesale measures are not in place. Discrimination, investigation is necessary. Some of modern thought must be refuted. The rest must be made subservient. But nothing in it can be ignored. He that is not with us is against us. Modern culture is a mighty force. It is either subservient to the gospel or else it is the deadliest enemy of the gospel. For making it subservient, religious emotion is not enough, intellectual labor is also necessary. And that labor is being neglected. The Church has turned to easier tasks. And now she is reaping the fruits of her indolence. Now she must battle for her life.

A Call to Battle

The situation is desperate. It might discourage us. But not if we are truly Christians. Not if we are living in vital communion with the risen Lord. If we are really convinced of the truth of our message, then we can proclaim it before a world of enemies, then the very difficulty of our task, the very scarcity of our allies becomes an inspiration, then we can even rejoice that God did not place us in an easy age, but in a time of doubt and perplexity and battle. Then, too, we shall not be afraid to call forth other soldiers into the conflict. Instead of making our theological seminaries merely centers of religious emotion, we shall make them battle-grounds of the faith, where, helped a little by the experience of Christian teachers, men are taught to fight their own battle, where they come to appreciate the real strength of the adversary and in the hard school of intellectual struggle learn to substitute for the unthinking faith of childhood the profound convictions of full-grown men. Let us not fear in this a loss of spiritual power. The Church is perishing today through the lack of thinking, not through an excess of it. She is winning victories in the sphere of material betterment. Such victories are glorious. God save us from the heartless crime of disparaging them. They are relieving the misery of men. But if they stand alone, I fear they are but temporary. The things which are seen are temporal; the things which are not seen are eternal. What will become of philanthropy if God be lost? Beneath the surface of life lies a world of spirit. Philosophers have attempted to explore it. Christianity has revealed its wonders to the simple soul. There lie the springs of the Church's power. But that spiritual realm cannot be entered without controversy. And now the Church is shrinking from the conflict. Driven from the spiritual realm by the current of modern thought, she is consoling herself with things about which there is no dispute. If she favors better housing for the poor, she need fear no contradiction. She will need all her courage. She will have enemies enough, God knows. But they will not fight her with argument. The twentieth century, in theory, is agreed on social betterment. But sin, and death, and salvation, and life, and God— about these things there is debate. You can avoid the debate if you choose. You need only drift with the current. Preach every Sunday during your Seminary course, devote the fag ends of your time to study and to thought, study about as you studied in college—and these questions will probably never trouble you. The great questions may easily be avoided. Many preachers are avoiding them. And many preachers are preaching to the air. The Church is waiting for men of another type. Men to fight her battles and solve her problems. The hope of finding them is the one great inspiration of a Seminary's life. They need not all be men of conspicuous attainments. But they must all be men of thought. They must fight hard against spiritual and intellectual indolence. Their thinking may be confined to narrow limits. But it must be their own. To them theology must be something more than a task. It must be a matter of inquiry. It must lead not to successful memorizing, but to genuine convictions.

The Church is puzzled by the world's indifference. She is trying to overcome it by adapting her message to the fashions of the day. But if, instead, before the conflict, she would descend into the secret place of meditation, if by the clear light of the gospel she would seek an answer not merely to the questions of the hour but, first of all, to the eternal problems of the spiritual world, then perhaps, by God's grace, through His good Spirit, in His good time, she might issue forth once more with power, and an age of doubt might be followed by the dawn of an era of faith.

CONCLUSION

I started by saying that you've been cheated. Many adults responsible for your education have not given you the tools to succeed. Having read this far in this book, I end by saying that you've been empowered. No matter your latent academic ability, if you follow these suggested study skills you will be in a position to maximize your potential academically. It is not what you *know* that will transform you, but what you *do*. To succeed, you will need to put these suggestions into practice. At first, it can be overwhelming. But if over the course of one nine-month academic year you concentrate on one chapter each month, by the end of the year you will be a transformed student. I believe in you and I believe in the study skills outlined here.

You don't have too much of a choice about being in school. If you are struggling, if you are failing, it is inevitably a drag. It doesn't have to be that way. School can be fun and rewarding—though one does not get there without some effort. No one likes to feel like a loser. As someone who has felt like a loser, I can honestly say it doesn't have to be that way. You can turn your academic career around. You can feel better about yourself. You can succeed.

It is for this reason that I wrote this book for you. Don't be overwhelmed. Take little steps; plan for incremental victories. But start today, because you have a responsibility to yourself and God to maximize all your God-given potential. There is far more potential there than you realize. Make mastering these study skills the great adventure of your school years and as a byproduct you will get an education as well.

In the spirit of praying before doing your homework, let's end with this Anglican prayer for education from *The Book of Common Prayer*,

> *Almighty God, the fountain of all wisdom: Enlighten by thy Holy Spirit those who teach and those who learn, that, rejoicing in the knowledge of thy truth, they may worship thee and serve thee from generation to generation; through Jesus Christ our Lord, who liveth and reigneth with thee and the same Spirit, one God, for ever and ever. Amen.*

ABOUT THE AUTHOR

David John Seel, Jr. is a writer and cultural analyst. He is the son of medical missionaries to South Korea, where he lived for seventeen years. He was homeschooled and attended a missionary boarding school. He has a triple major from Austin College: business administration, history, and philosophy. After serving as an Inter-Varsity Christian Fellowship staff member at Texas Southern University, Rice University, and Texas A&M University, Seel attended Covenant Theological Seminary where he received a M.Div. degree. He never intended to be ordained, simply a theologically equipped layman. He went on to get a doctorate in American Studies at the University of Maryland (College Park), where he focused on the social science analysis of Pierre Bourdieu.

Seel began his professional career as the Vice President of Client Services for the John Naisbitt Group. He spent fifteen years working closely with Os Guinness as the administrative director of the Williamsburg Charter and later co-founded with Guinness the Trinity Forum.

Seel taught Bible and European history at the Stony Brook School and served as the administrative director and research professor at the Institute for Advanced Studies in Culture at the University of Virginia. He is the founding headmaster of the Cambridge School of Dallas, where he also served as crew coach. He was a founding board member of the Society for Classical Learning and the Council on Educational Standards & Accountability. Most recently, Seel served as the director of cultural engagement at the John Templeton Foundation.

Upon leaving Templeton, Seel has devoted his time to writing and cultural engagement strategy and fundraising consulting. He is the author of *The New Copernicans: Millennials and the Survival of the Church* and *To Make a Difference: The Secret of Dense Networks*. He is a frequent contributor to *Critique* magazine and blogs at www.ncconversations.com.

He and his wife, Kathryn, live on a historic 250-year-old farm in Philadelphia with their English cream golden retriever, Malibu. They have three grown children and four grandchildren. They attend a Reformed Episcopal Church.

BIBLIOGRAPHY

William A. Armstrong. *Study Is Hard Work: The Most Accessible and Lucid Text Available on Assuming and Keeping Study Skills Through a Lifetime* (David R. Godine, 1995).

Mortimer J. Adler and Charles Van Doren. *How to Read a Book: The Classic Guide to Intelligent Reading* (Simon & Schuster, 1972).

Jacque Barzun. *Simple & Direct: A Rhetoric for Writers* (Harper Perennial, 1981)

Scott Crider. *The Office of Assertion: An Art of Rhetoric for the Academic Essay* (Intercollegiate Studies Institute, 2005).

Chip Heath and Dan Heath. *Made to Stick: Why Some Ideas Survive and Others Die* (Random House, 2007).

Tracy Lee Simmons. *Climbing Parnassus: A New Apologia for Greek and Latin* (Intercollegiate Studies Institute, 2007).

Made in the USA
Las Vegas, NV
24 August 2021

28799155R00094